VW BEETLE

THE GOLDEN YEARS 1949–1968

RICHARD COPPING

AMBERLEY

First published 2023

Amberley Publishing
The Hill, Stroud,
Gloucestershire, GL5 4EP

www.amberley-books.com

ISBN: 978 1 4456 8892 3 (print)
ISBN: 978 1 4456 8893 0 (ebook)

British Library Cataloguing in Publication Data.
A catalogue record for this book is available from the British Library.

Typeset in 10pt on 13pt Celeste.
Typesetting by SJmagic DESIGN SERVICES, India.
Printed in the UK.

Contents

Preface

An outrageously unfair tale of latter-day denials summarises the sixty-nine-year history of Volkswagen's legendary Sedan, better known as the *Käfer*, Beetle, Bug and *Fusca* among other names. Rightly heralded as the work of Ferdinand Porsche, little or nothing is said of his murky association with the Nazis until it was clear their cause was lost, or of their ownership of the vast factory built specifically for the Sedan's production. Many insist that it was British efforts in the immediate post-war years that ensured the car's future, despite the evidence of the desperate production numbers, dismal sales and a largely derelict, bomb-damaged factory, all of which are consistently overlooked. References to the enormous successes of the first post-war German Director General are constrained and his remarkable achievements played down. The Sedan and Heinz Nordhoff's detractors instead over-emphasise his final years in office, at a time when Germany was experiencing its first post-war recession. Inevitably, Sedan sales did fall temporarily, but these critics none too subtly link Volkswagen's decline following Nordhoff's death in April 1968 and the company's near bankruptcy in 1973/4 to him. If Nordhoff had abandoned the Sedan's cause

Heinz Nordhoff, Director General of Volkswagen, 1948–1968, alongside the car he inherited and developed to become the phenomenon it will always remain.

many moons previously, and long before in excess of one million cars per annum were leaving Wolfsburg and some of VW's other factories, all would have been well they declare. Finally, still not satisfied, the self-same cynics extol the VW Golf's undoubted success at the expense of the car that had taken the Model T Ford's crown as the most produced single model in automotive history. Yes, a series of cars of varying designs and proportions carrying the name VW Golf when amalgamated into one to trounce the Beetle's single model total, just as even more versions of the Toyota Corolla continue to eclipse the sum total of eight different VW Golfs. However, no manufacturer has produced or is likely ever to produce the Beetle's record-breaking total of 21,529,464 examples of a single type. Why bury this remarkable feat in the sand?

The aim of this book is to recount the Sedan's glory years, the period between 1948 and 1968 when Heinz Nordhoff was at the helm, but in so doing it is essential to revisit the period before his twenty years at Volkswagen and both the four years of mismanagement following his death and the further thirty when the Beetle still played a significant role somewhere in the world.

The car Volkswagen's Director General inherited in 1948 and the model he left twenty years later. Changes minor, more major, and often technical; these were the new models of the Nordhoff era and the reason why the VW we know as the Beetle has held the record as the most produced car of a single type since 1972.

1

Origins: Ferdinand Porsche and the Nazis (1933–1945)

In February 1933 the newly elected Chancellor of Germany addressed those attending the annual Berlin Motor Show. Concerned about the lack of car ownership in the state when compared to many other developed countries, he spoke of reducing car taxes, relaxing oppressive traffic laws and the need to make it far easier to acquire a driving licence. He also outlined his proposals to build an unrivalled road system, the German Autobahn network, and of the pressing need to assist the many who relied on a motorcycle as their only means of transport to be able to buy a small car at a realistic price.

The words of Adolf Hitler were pure gold dust to the brilliant, but highly temperamental, designer, Ferdinand Porsche, a man whose reputation lay in the field of creating groundbreaking, high-powered cars. However, for many years the fifty-eight-year-old had dreamed of creating a *Volksauto*, or *Kleinauto* – a small car for ordinary Germans. Indeed, as early as 1900 he had experimented with just such a car, but this and subsequent projects each fell by the wayside. Porsche's fiery temper, boardroom struggles, or a company's financial collapse, were the root causes. By 1931, with no desire to be thwarted again in this ambition or any other, Porsche decided to set up his own design studio.

The partnership: Adolf Hitler (seated) and Ferdinand Porsche (stood by their car and surrounded by high-ranking Nazi officers).

To his evident delight, Porsche was soon commissioned by Fritz Neumeyer of the motorcycle manufacturing company Zündapp Gmbh to produce a *Kleinauto*. The car that quickly began to take shape was the first to carry both a visual and mechanical resemblance to the future Volkswagen Sedan; its engine, although water-cooled, as Neumeyer believed that air-cooled engines were too noisy, was at the rear and it featured Porsche's recently patented torsion bar suspension. Sadly,, for Neumeyer, both regular engine overheating issues and torsion bars that shattered with frequent monotony spelled caution and when he discovered the cost of the necessary stamping presses required to form the final steel body, he duly cancelled the project.

However, all was not completely lost, as in 1933 Porsche was approached by the head of NSU, Fritz von Falkenhayn, with a view to taking the *Kleinauto* project further steps forward. It is likely that Porsche had made the necessary modifications to the Zündapp vehicle in his own time, and at his own expense, as the prototypes prepared for NSU appeared unrealistically quickly. As before, torsion bars were a key feature of the vehicle's make-up, with trailing arms at the front and swing axles at the rear. The engine was mounted at the rear as per the Zündapp car, but this time, as was Porsche's preference, it was air-cooled. Developing a maximum of 26 PS (metric brake-horsepower), the 1470cc flat-four offered its top speed at just 2,600 rpm. The Sedan was destined to follow in the same vein. Frustratingly, once again Porsche was destined to be thwarted. Growing concerns about raising the necessary investment to build the proposed car, coupled to the buoyancy of motorcycle sales and the consequent lack of the necessary capacity to

Hitler was chauffeured at the factory foundation-laying ceremony by Porsche's son, Ferry.

manufacture an additional vehicle, were both serious. However the killer blow came from the Italian manufacturer Fiat. After becoming aware of Porsche's latest commission, they speedily reminded NSU of an agreement signed between the two whereby the German company would never build a four-wheeled vehicle under its own name.

Following Hitler's speech at the Berlin Motor Show, Porsche scurried away full of enthusiasm for presenting the Reich Ministry of Transport with a design portfolio for the construction of a *Kleinauto.* On this occasion good fortune played into his hands. One Jakob Werlin had sold Hitler his first Mercedes more than a decade previously. At the time Porsche worked for Daimler Benz and the two men became acquainted. Werlin carefully retained his influence in the Nazi court over the following years, offering advice whenever it was sought. Now, having visited Porsche and learned of his small car ambitions, Werlin reported back to the Führer, who, having met the designer in the context of an Auto Union Racing Project, immediately wished to see him again. Exactly when the two men met is unclear but there is a distinct possibility that the get-together took place in late August, or early September 1933. Hitler apparently spoke at length and with knowledgeable detail. The car he wanted should be able to seat a family of two adults and three children, must be economical to run, but should not be of the three-wheeler class. While Hitler expressed his preference for a *Volks Wagen,* or car for the German *Volk* (literally folk, but in the Nazi era more closely associated with nationalism and the soul of the German people) with its engine at the front, he made it clear that he was not averse to a rear-mounted power plant, one that might even run on diesel. The only immovable demand that Porsche found it near impossible to contemplate was that the car should retail below 1,000 Reichsmarks, less than half the proposed prices for both the Zündapp and NSU vehicles, though had the war not intervened it is believed that the Nazi car would have been subsidised to sell at 1,000 Reichsmarks in 1939. More significantly still, Hitler's demand drove Porsche to produce a quality product at minimal price.

Just a few months later, on 17 January 1934, Porsche duly presented his Exposé, a masterpiece carefully crafted to mirror Hitler's wishes. Any notion of producing a car with smaller than average dimensions at the expense of handling and life expectancy was dismissed. However, the overall weight would be comparatively low, and it would have the necessary power to achieve normal maximum speeds and climbing abilities. Passenger space would be a prime consideration, while unnecessarily complicated equipment would be avoided, thus reducing servicing to an absolute minimum.

To achieve such requirements, Porsche wrote of the best possible suspension and handling, a maximum speed in the region of 100 kph, a climbing ability of around thirty per cent, a closed full four-seat body for the passengers, the lowest possible purchase price and last, but not least, the most economical of running costs. Such a specification demanded a wheelbase of 2,500 mm and a track of 1,200 mm to accommodate a possible five occupants, an engine developing a maximum of 26 PS at a lowly 3,500 rpm to ensure necessary power and life expectancy, and a kerb weight of 650 kg, which would ensure economical average fuel consumption of 8 litres per 100 km. A full swing-axle was also suggested. Porsche's only deviation from total subservience to Hitler's demands was to suggest that a car of this calibre would command a price of 1,550 Reichsmarks.

Shortly after presenting his Exposé, Porsche was informed that the RDA (the Reich Association of the German Automobile Industry), would be working with him to produce

The enormous factory built specifically for production of Hitler and Porsche's car was owned by the Nazi Party. Porsche and key Nazis directed operations.

a *Volksauto.* The reluctant trade association of German car manufacturers had no choice in the matter, as Hitler made abundantly clear at the 1934 Berlin Motor Show:

> Germany has only one automobile for every one hundred of its people. France on the other hand has one for each twenty-eight, while the USA has one for every six of its citizens. That disparity will be changed. I wish to see a mass-produced German-built car that can be bought by anyone who has the income to afford a motorbike ... We must have a real car for the German people – a *Volkswagen.*

Porsche's contract gave him six months to design the car fully and just a further four to build one prototype. He was told that the car must sell at 900 Reichsmarks. By December 1934 Porsche had been granted permission to build three prototypes and by 1936 this V series (as it is now known) had increased to five examples. Crucially, these earliest of prototypes bore more than a passing resemblance to the production Sedan of a few years later. Extensive and largely unprecedented testing took place, the result of which was a further series of prototypes, thirty in number, designated W30. These were tested by carefully selected members of the SS and including the costs of the 1.95 million kilometres travelled by these cars, the total bill for them was a staggering 1.7 million Reichsmarks. Still more prototypes followed, most notably the VW38 (a reference to the year in which they were built). Rather than incorporating drastic changes made in the light of earlier testing, these cars were largely promotional vehicles, with publicity tours starting in the autumn of 1938. By now the differences between the pre-war vehicle Hitler had named the 'Strength Through Joy' car (*Kraft durch Freude,* or KdF-Wagen, in deference to the division of the Nazi established *Deutsche Arbeitsfront* (German Labour Front) devoted to instructional leisure activities), and the post-war Sedan were almost non-existent.

Perhaps more significantly still, the KdF-Wagen was completely entwined with the Nazi Party and Hitler's Third Reich. The car would have not reached the production stage without them, their money, appropriated or otherwise, and Hitler's ruthless determination.

Deliberate but ill-advised procrastination by members of the RDA to what they saw as a potential rival to their own products, came to a head at the time of the Berlin Motor Show in 1937. Naively, Adam Opel showed the Führer his new small car, the P4, marketed as 'the car of the little man.' Hitler stormed away, furious that anyone dared to challenge his car with a product of their own. His speech, spat out at the show, was loaded with barely disguised threats:

> Let there be no doubt – so-called private business is either capable of dealing with this issue or it is not competent to continue as private business. The National Socialist State will under no circumstances capitulate to the convenience, the limitations, or the ill-will of individual Germans.

Shortly afterwards, Opel and others found it increasingly difficult to obtain the materials necessary to build cars such as the P4. Then, when it was leaked that Opel planned to cut the price of their small saloon, menacing messages were despatched posthaste indicating that such cuts would not be tolerated.

Cover of the Nazi-produced elaborate brochure to sell the vehicle Hitler had named the Strength Through Joy car. The stamps depicted relate to a savings scheme which fell foul of wartime activity.

Reluctance, bordering on open hostility, on the part of the manufacturers to the idea of handing over assembly lines in their factories to production of the *Volks Wagen* or supplying parts and panels for the *Kleinauto,* produced drastic if not unexpected consequences. Hitler, with the financial security of the nation's wealth at his disposal, decreed that the Nazi party would found a company for the specific purpose of manufacturing the car. The board of management of the *Gesellschaft zur Vorbereitung des Volkswagens* consisted of Hitler's 'friend' Jakob Werlin, Bodo Lafferentz (a committed Nazi and assistant to Robert Ley, the head of the German Labour Front) and the apparently none too innocent or naive Ferdinand Porsche. Their task was to ensure that, in ten years, 1.5 million cars would be built annually. In order to achieve that target a factory, which would be the largest in Europe, would be built.

Needless to say, land was requisitioned without thought for the inhabitants of the locality. To give a sense of the scale of the undertaking, at the outbreak of war four massive halls had been built plus an all-important power station. Hall One took the form of a tool and die shop covering 420,000 sq ft; Hall Two was a Press Shop of 447,000 sq ft; Hall Three, at 775,000 sq ft, was the largest and devoted to a combination of paint shop, body framing and final assembly. Hall Four, committed to the machining of parts and the completion of mechanical sub-assemblies, was the second largest at 527,000 sq ft. Perhaps

A crocodile of prototypes invades Berlin and the Brandenburg Gate in 1938.

most impressive of all was the fact that the factory frontage extended to 1,350 metres, or three-quarters of a mile.

Only the intervention of war stopped the Nazis achieving their plan for mass production of the KdF-Wagen: between 1939 and the end of the war, very few Strength Through Joy cars were built, the factory's production and Porsche's attention being turned over to military incarnations of the car in the form of the *Kübelwagen* (a sort of German Jeep using largely KdF components), the more niche but self-explanatory Schwimmwagen, plus four-wheel-drive versions of the saloon and other projects. According to one source, May 1944 proved a high point with production of 1,800 *Kübels,* 1,000 Schwimmwagens, 1,200 V-1 bombs, 100,000 mines and the repair of 30 Junker-88s.

1941 saw 41 genuine KdF-Wagens built at Wolfsburg, to be followed by 157 in 1942. By the high summer of 1944 just 630 cars that could not be mistaken for military vehicles had been produced. None were available to German citizens, instead being channelled to Nazi dignitaries, friends of the Party or, in the case of the Emperor Hirohito of Japan, wartime allies.

Above: The centrefold of the handbook serves to confirm that the Nazi car and examples built many years later were one and the same vehicle. The red lines guide the browser to specific details of the car's make up.

Right: Cover of the Nazi-produced KdF-Wagen handbook, a well-detailed and illustrated thorough guide to the car.

2

British adhoc Ingenuity (1945–1947)

It was American troops who liberated the KdF factory workforce on 12 April 1945, a population largely made up of forced labour, including Poles and Russians who, once the Nazis had buried their uniforms and run for their lives, ran amok for a full five days of devastation. However, amid a mass of tangled girders, roofs open to the sky and serious water ingress, indeed sixty-five per cent total destruction attributable to bombing, plus telephones ripped from the walls and typewriters smashed as part of the general campaign of ruin, one vital component of the factory's make-up survived. Thanks to the efforts of the town's mayor and the dedicated work of its manager, the power plant continued to heat one and all, including the residents of the largely wooden settlement across the Mittelland Canal.

In the Allies' planned division of the former Nazi state, Wolfsburg, as it was soon referred to, fell into the British sector of occupation. They duly arrived in mid-May and in August 1945 a REME Major, Yorkshireman Ivan Hirst, was sent to Wolfsburg with no specific orders other than to take control. At the risk of over-simplifying the initial weeks and months of British

Major Ivan Hirst, the officer sent to the former KdF factory in August 1945 with no specific orders other than to take control and without whose ingenuity the revival in the car's fortunes may not have been possible.

Much of the factory had suffered significant bomb damage, making working conditions difficult, especially if it rained.

occupation, rumblings about the future of the once Nazi Party owned and consequently now ownerless factory were at the forefront, while the need for transport for the Allies almost by accident set a path that went a considerable way to securing the *Volksauto's* future.

Dealing with the latter first, inevitably the military preference was for Hirst to build *Kübelwagens*, but this was not to be. In 1938, as part of his research visit to the USA, a project involving the Nazi sympathiser Henry Ford among others, Porsche had met representatives of the Budd Corporation, sheet metal fabricators and major suppliers of automotive components. He came away with the rights to make an all-steel body for his car using Budd techniques under licence. For their part, Budd, whose tentacles extended to a factory in Berlin, were granted the right to make the bodies for the first KdF derivative, which it was thought would be the relatively niche market soft-top version of the saloon. Taking into account that when Porsche began to build the *Kübelwagen* at the KdF factory, America and Germany were not at war, Budd insisted on producing the bodies, as had been agreed. Thus, complete bodyshells were sent from Budd's operation in Berlin by rail to the KdF factory.

During the latter stages of the war bomb damage to the Ambi Budd works was severe, some even say total. However, this was largely academic in 1945, as what remained of the factory was placed in Soviet hands and the Russians immediately dismantled what was left of the press and body plant and ferried anything useful back to their homeland.

Hirst's initial commanding officer was Colonel Michael McEvoy, who was based at Rhine Army Headquarters. This was fortuitous, for wealth inherited by the Colonel had allowed him to establish McEvoy Racing Motorcycles, an organisation that during the 1930s went on to produce conversions on popular vehicles and supercharging. A true professional, he was acting as a consultant to Mercedes when he'd visited the 1939 Berlin Motor Show. Here he'd come across and already evaluated the much boasted about KdF-Wagen.

Without the *Kübelwagen's* availability McEvoy suggested making use of the Sedan. Hirst managed to find an abandoned one in the depths of the factory, had it tidied up and re-spayed Khaki Green and despatched it to the Colonel. With dexterity McEvoy demonstrated it both to the ranks of the British Army of the Rhine and the CCG (Control Commission for Germany). Again at the risk of simplification, the CCG soon requested 5,000 *Volkswagens* (the term KdF-Wagen having being wiped from memory), and this number was quickly extended to 20,000.

Manufacture proved far from easy, but the car couldn't have been in better hands than those of the super-enthusiastic and gifted amateur Ivan Hirst. A qualified optician, he ran his own workshop dedicated to the repair of optical instruments until he was called up. Now he threw the skills he'd acquired into solving the tricky issues preventing straight-forward manufacture of the car officially known now as the Volkswagen.

For example, Hirst had to act quickly and open a foundry, following the abrupt closure of the factory making both crankcases and transmission housings due to the majority of

During March 1946 a first production target was reached. To the right of the picture Hirst stands between Wing Commander Berryman and Rudolph Brörmann, the German manager whose associations with the Nazis forced his dismissal.

their business having been associated with the aircraft industry. Similarly, a lack of sheets of steel large enough to create a roof panel resulted in Hirst ordering a butt welder to be designed and built, so that one large sheet of steel could be created out of two smaller ones. Perhaps best of all, if the aim is to illustrate Hirst's ingenuity, is to relay the tale of a lack of available carburettors, as previously made by Pierburg in Berlin to a design licensed by Solex. Hirst proceeded to strip a remaining example down on his desk, dividing the components that could be made at the factory from those that couldn't. The smaller brass parts were quickly taken to the camera firm of Voigtländer in nearby Brunswick, who agreed to recreate items such as the float and jets. Meanwhile, an alternate carburettor body was developed within the factory as gravity die castings worked in aluminium.

Running alongside the story of tooling shortages, a lack of materials and the rather dubious nature of the finished product with doors that didn't shut properly, headlamp lenses that cracked when the vehicle was in motion, and, most serious of all, premature rusting due to the quality of the paint finish, was the question of the now ownerless factory's future.

The Allies' Potsdam conference of 17 July to 2 August 1945 imposed the severest of measures on what remained of German industry. Manufacturing and services were only to be maintained to a level required by the occupying powers and displaced people, although a modest standard of living for the vanquished citizens of Germany was to be offered. Any business, or building, in excess of such basics was to be dismantled or destroyed. The former KdF factory, which had in its existence been almost entirely devoted to the production of goods related to the war, was duly listed for destruction. However, there was a potential degree of ambiguity in the ruling. The British Control Commission recognised that the factory had genuinely been built with the intention of producing cars. The Level of Industry Plan for Germany deemed that any factory not in operation in 1938 would count as part of the war preparations effort. As a result, the Wolfsburg Motor Works was not designated a war plant to be levelled as though it had never existed, but instead listed as surplus to requirements for the level of industry allowed and thus available for reparations.

There followed a series of reports and experts, each of which announced, to all those who might have been interested in stripping the factory of its assets, that within its walls there was little of value. For example, the commission of which William Rootes was head decreed that the Volkswagen 'did not meet the fundamental technical requirements of a motor car'. Humber Engineering declared that they 'did not consider that the design represents any special brilliance', while AC Cars believed that 'the designer had given just enough but no more', and 'as a civilian vehicle considerable modification would be required to conform to the standard expected'.

At face value the situation for both the Volkswagen and its latest mentor was going from bad to worse. Henry Ford was alleged to have said that he would not have the car, or the rights to it, as a gift. After sending a small team to look at the plant Australia quickly backed away. France's Communist Minister of Industry's interest rapidly evaporated. In reality, the rejection of the car by all and sundry was good news for Hirst and others. Despite its shoddy nature, demand for the car from the CCG and the British Armed forces remained strong. In March 1946, for the first time a total of 1,000 cars were built during the course of the month. In 1945, just 1,785 cars had been built, but the following year this figure escalated to 10,020, while in September any thoughts of dismantling the factory were put on hold for the next four years. In October the plan which limited production of automobiles to 40,000 across Germany was also duly revised.

Almost by a fluke the Volkswagen appeared to have a way forward. It was becoming increasingly apparent to many, Ivan Hirst being a possible exception, that it was not the intention of the British to retain control or custodianship of the factory and fledgling business. To secure a successful transfer it was necessary to recruit an automotive professional, a German with the necessary drive, understanding of automated methods and experience to run Volkswagen. The choice of candidate made was to herald Volkswagen's first golden age.

3

De Luxe Beetles

> I remember thinking when I first saw the factory that it looked just as it must have done after the last bomb had exploded in it...

Those were the words of Heinz Nordhoff, as spoken to the author Walter Henry Nelson for the book *Small Wonder*, first published in 1967. The task that faced the newly appointed forty-nine-year-old Director General of the vast Wolfsburg factory was enormous, one that would require dedication to the cause over and above any rational call to duty, and demand a level of professionalism and expertise that few others would have been capable of providing. Those involved in Nordhoff's appointment were extremely lucky that a quirk of fate brought him to Wolfsburg, when under earlier circumstances any such advance on their part would have been rebuffed with alacrity.

1949 saw the launch of the De Luxe, or Export, model. Externally, a high-quality gloss paint finish was accompanied by a shiny trim package in keeping with the standards of the day.

Before arriving at Volkswagen's far from hallowed portals at the beginning of 1948, Heinz Nordhoff had worked first for BMW (as an aircraft designer) and then for fifteen years at Opel. At the latter he graduated from the role of department head within the service organisation, to being a technical consultant to the company's sales managers. On more than one occasion he was invited to the USA and General Motors (who took full control of the German firm in 1931). His task was to immerse himself in the sophistication and cost-saving automation of their production methods. Versed in the most modern methodology, by the end of the 1930s Nordhoff had deservedly been appointed to the Opel Board of Management. In the early months of 1939, he transferred to Berlin to direct Opel's operations from there. A little over three years later, he was appointed Director General of the Brandenburg factory, then the largest lorry manufacturing plant in Europe.

However, at the end of the war Opel's operations lay in the American zone and under their rules of de-Nazification, Nordhoff, who had never been a member of, or sympathetic to, the Nazi party, was dismissed, as he held the rank of *Wehrwirtschaftsführer*, a relatively minor honour awarded in respect of the contribution he'd made to the war effort through his work in the motor industry. Temporarily assisting the widow of an Opel franchisee in

Inside the new De Luxe Volkswagen. Simple to implement and effective – fittings changed from everyday black to an executive ivory colour. The steering wheel looked less industrial in its two-spoke presentation. The radio was an extra cost item, but cars not fitted with one possessed a neat blanking panel. Previously, adding a radio would have meant use of a hacksaw.

Hamburg to support his family, Nordhoff was both free and eager to take up the reins of any challenge presented to him.

Addressing an audience in Zurich in 1954, Nordhoff recalled how on his arrival at Wolfsburg he was 'faced with a desolate heap of rubble, a horde of desperate people, the torso of a deserted town – an unstructured mass which had never had any organising principle, no factory organisation in the real sense, lacking a programme or any rational work organisation.' To conclude his address Nordhoff had stated that 'something new had to be created because there was nothing there and never had been anything to build on at all.'

In 1958, on the occasion of his accepting America's prestigious Elmer A. Sperry award, Nordhoff elaborated on previous utterances, systematically detailing the difficulties he'd faced, starting with the state of the factory:

> I had to start from scratch in the real sense of the word. Seven thousand workers were painfully producing six thousand cars a year, provided it did not rain too much. Most of the roof and all of the windows of the factory had been destroyed. Pools of stagnant water were under foot...

Otto Höhne, who had joined the staff of the KdF factory on 1 June 1939 and who later held high office in Nordhoff's court, confirmed how when the new Director General arrived 'assembly line workers stood in water up over their ankles when it rained. Some of them

A woollen headlining that extended to the base of the side and rear windows and luxury seating set the De Luxe apart from earlier cars. The bolster cushions though were quickly deemed to be over the top and were dispensed with in November 1951.

had to work outside and were protected only by a makeshift sheet-metal "roof". We had to keep fires burning near the machines so the hydraulic fluid wouldn't freeze.'

The only way to undertake the urgent factory refurbishment required was to generate sufficient income to afford wholesale activity. Three intrinsically linked major challenges stood in the way. Years later Nordhoff recounted to the German news magazine *Der Spiegel* that 'tremendously risky decisions had to be taken, production had to be stepped up to an unheard of level, the export market had to be opened to an extent never before imagined.' However, to meet either of those targets, problems with the car itself and how much it was costing to build had to be addressed.

Nordhoff explained to his audience at the Sperry award:

> When I assumed the responsibility of putting this wrecked factory into high volume production, the car itself was still 'full of bugs'. It really was what you call an 'ugly duckling.'
>
> ...At this time, nearly three years after the end of the war, 109.6 men were required to produce one car per day ... There was so much to be done. Weak points in the design had to be ironed out, bottlenecks in production had to be broken, and problems of material procurement, quality control, personnel had to be solved. There was no sales organisation ... and I was determined that, of all things, Volkswagen should have the best service in the world.

Under Hirst's necessarily ad hoc way of working, the outlay involved in building a single car could only be estimated, as there was a distinct suspicion that one vehicle might cost considerably more or less than both its predecessor and successor. In the same vein, it was rumoured that on average a single car took between three and four hundred hours to build.

Addressing the workforce during his first year in office, Nordhoff was brutally frank. 'Things cannot continue in this way', he announced. 'For the first time in its history, the

Two soft-top versions of the Sedan were also launched in 1949. Both were built by coachbuilders, allowing the factory to concentrate on the volume market. The Hebmüller depicted was short-lived, a fire at their workshops and subsequent financial troubles bringing production to a permanent halt.

Volkswagenwerk will this year have to face the necessity of standing on its own two feet.' Previous practices could not be allowed to persist for 'if we continue in this manner we shall not continue for long. We must reach 100 hours per car.' In the Sperry speech, with the benefit of several years' production under his belt, Nordhoff could offer the same message in a striking way: 'Nearly three years after the end of the war, 109.6 men were required to produce one car per day. Today [in 1958] this is figure is seventeen point nine.'

As for the car, Nordhoff was fulsome in his praise of Porsche; defects apparent were not of his making. 'There is ... [an] eternal debt to the engineering genius of Professor Ferdinand Porsche. He ... created an exceptionally fine and outstanding design that has been the basis for my own work ... and which ... [will be] the keystone of one of the greatest success stories in automobile history.'

In 1948 Wolfsburg produced 19,244 cars; this number escalated to 46,154 in 1949 and from there, in 1950 and 1951, to 81,979 and 93,709 respectively. Crucially, export sales grew from around fifteen per cent of the total in 1949, to over thirty per cent the following year. While currency reform in 1948 had helped kick-start the German economy generally, at Volkswagen it was Nordhoff's introduction of the De Luxe, or Export, model on 1 July 1949 that transformed its fortunes. Porsche's structural and mechanical recipe remained unaltered; the extremely basic and generally dubious standard of finish accepted by the British, and which Nordhoff had started to work on almost from day one, was banished forever.

The appeal of the De Luxe ensured that sales figures began to escalate dramatically and the 100,000th post-war car rolled off the assembly line on 4 March 1950. Nearly fifty per cent of the total had been produced in 1949.

A serious contender

Mechanically and structurally identical to Sedans of previous years, from 1 July 1949 two separate models were available. The Standard model bore a close resemblance to the car produced in the British era, offering the most spartan of trim levels, both externally and internally. Realistically, this car was aimed at a percentage of the home market that was driven by price rather than any other consideration, the difference between the two models amounting to 650DM. However, its basic constitution overlooked, the Standard model no longer suffered from the defects alluded to by Nordhoff in his Sperry speech and elsewhere.

As for the specification of the De Luxe, overnight the car became a serious contender where Nordhoff chose to send it, whereas previously it was unlikely to proceed past the first hurdle. Externally, the De Luxe model benefited from a high-gloss paint finish available in a variety of shades. It also profited from the presence of chrome – with bumpers, door handles, headlamp rims and hubcaps finished to a high standard in this way. It gained a boot lid mounted VW roundel, while the lower sections of both front wings attracted a small circular grill. One of these was a blanking panel, included purely for aesthetic balance; the other, which perforated the wing's metal, allowed the sound of the horn to be heard clearly following its relocation behind the wing rather than being clumsily exposed on the bumper bracket. Brightwork trim was also to be found on the car's swage line, the spine of the boot lid and even the lower edge of the running boards.

For ladies who lunch. Here was a limousine ideal as transport for a wide selection of people both at home and abroad *c.* 1952. Note the boot-lid badge and the shiny trim surrounding the windscreen.

Inside, the De Luxe demonstrated luxury with a full woollen headlining (compared to the Standard model's small square of cloth and large areas of painted metal), much improved upholstery and trim panels, grab handles for rear seat passengers and the replacement of all black fittings with the more upmarket and noticeable shade of ivory. The steering wheel, also finished in ivory, was of a new less mundane two-spoke design (the Standard model retaining the old commercial vehicle-like three-spoke affair).

Behind the scenes, the De Luxe had the decided benefit of better soundproofing materials in the engine compartment, while the front seats were fitted with spring-loaded adjusting handles for fore and aft movement (rather than relying on dexterity with wing nuts). Likewise, facilities were included to alter the rake of the backrests, while hard-wearing cord trim made the luggage area behind the back seat far more durable.

Specs from a November 1952 Volkswagen Sedan brochure

Engine

- Design: 4 cylinder 4 cycle engine in rear of car
- Arrangement of cylinders: horizontally opposed
- Bore: 75 mm
- Stroke: 64 mm
- Capacity: 1,131 cm^3 (until 1943 985cc)
- Compression ratio: 5.8:1
- Valves: overhead
- Maximum PS: 24 at 3,000 rpm
- Piston speed: 6.42 m/s at 3,000 rpm
- Carburettor: downdraft type Solex 28 PCI
- Cooling system: air cooling by fan, automatically regulated by thermostat
- Battery: 6 volts
- Generator: Bosch RED k 130/6 – 2600 Al 16, with voltage regulator
- Clutch: single disc, dry (Fichtel & Sachs)
- Transmission: 4 forward speeds, 1 reverse
- Gear Ratios: First 1:3.60, Second 1: 1.88, third 1: 1.22, top 1: 0.79, reverse 1 : 4.63
- second, third and fourth gears synchronised and silent (De Luxe only – from 01 10 1952)
- Rear axle drive: power is transmitted through helically cut drive pinion and ring gear, via two swinging axles to rear wheels

General

- Chassis: frame with channel-shaped centre section forked at the rear and welded-on platform
- Front axle: independent suspension through longitudinal upper and lower torsion arms, two square torsion bar springs passing through beams
- Rear axle: independent suspension through swinging half-axles with spring plates, one round torsion bar spring on each side

- Shock absorbers: double-acting hydraulic telescopic type, front and rear, requiring no attention
- Steering: special worm steering gear with divided track rod
- Turns of steering wheel (lock to lock): 2.4
- Turning circle: 10 m
- Tyres: 5.60 x 15 (prior to October 1952 – 5.00 x 16)
- Foot brake: hydraulic (Ate) operating on all four wheels (before May 1950 cable brakes. These were retained on the Standard model and would be throughout the 1950s and into the 1960s)
- Hand brake: mechanical, operating on rear wheels

Weights and measures
Length 4,050 mm, height 1,500 mm, width 1,540 mm
Ground clearance 212 mm
Wheelbase: 2,400 mm
Track width: front 1,290 mm, rear 1,250 mm
Dead weight: 775 kg
Empty weight (fuelled, with spare wheel and accessories): 800 kg
Permissible load: 360 kg
Permissible total weight: 1,160 kg
Performance (1950)
Fuel tank: 40 litres, of which 5 litres reserve
Fuel consumption: about 7.5 litres per 100 km (road consumption)
Climbing ability: in 1st gear 32%, in 2nd gear 18%, in 3rd gear 9%, in 4th gear 5%
Maximum and continuous speed: 100 km/h at 3,000 rpm

One stage further – was it realistic to suggest that guests staying at the Savoy would arrive in a Volkswagen Sedan? *c.* 1952.

Further details

Distortion-proof all-steel body with high lustre, weatherproof synthetic resin finish. Sound deadening of the interior through improved insulation around the engine compartment is achieved through additional soundproof plates and through a sound-absorbing coat on the frame fork. Turning knob for fine adjustment of heating. Free moving and well-geared window winder. Door trimming with imitation leather kick pad. Mouldings at both inner sides. Built-in ash tray also in rear compartment. Door pocket beside driver's seat. Interior light at left-hand side above door lock pillar. Rubber mats secured to the floor by patent fasteners. Improved seat springs and higher seat backs for better shoulder support. Surprisingly large luggage capacity behind rear seat and under bonnet.

Volkswagen clearly thought the Standard model depicted had a role to play. Posing here as a travelling salesman's transport, how many sales executives today would be happy to arrive at their destination in a car with wing nuts to adjust the front seats? *c*. 1952.

4

Exporting the Beetle

At the risk of stealing a little of the thunder of the story of the millionth Beetle, the thirty-eight-page booklet produced to accompany the celebrations held in August 1955 included a list of all the countries the car had successfully invaded. A month over six years after launching the De Luxe, or Export, Sedan, Nordhoff had been successful in selling in the region of 420,000 cars to 109 countries across all continents, with the exception of

In 1949 the ever-enthusiastic Dutchman Ben Pon (left) was sent by Nordhoff to sell the Sedan to the USA. Despite his known talent in such a direction, America rejected the car en masse.

Antarctica. Inevitably, there were more countries to come, while sales figures were set to escalate dramatically in some nations.

Europe
Andorra - Belgium - Denmark - Finland - Gibraltar - Greece - Great Britain - Ireland - Iceland - Italy - Yugoslavia - Luxemburg - Malta - Netherlands - Norway - Austria - Portugal - Saarland (incorporated into Germany after French occupation in 1957) - Sweden - Switzerland - Spain - Free Territory of Trieste. (330,000 cars sold).

North and South America
Argentina - Barbados - Bermuda - Bolivia - Brazil - Chile - Costa Rico - Cuba - Curaçao - Dominican Republic - Ecuador - El Salvador - Guadeloupe - Guatemala - Haiti - Hawaii - Honduras - Jamaica - Canada - Antilles - Columbia - Martinique - Mexico - Nicaragua - Guyana - Panama - Paraguay - Peru - Puerto Rico - Trinidad - Uruguay - USA - Venezuela. (57,000 cars sold).

Africa
Egypt - Algeria - Ethiopia - Belgian Congo -Eritrea - French Morocco - French West Africa - Gold Coast - Canary Islands - Kenya - Liberia - Nigeria - Portuguese East Africa - Portuguese West Africa - Réunion Island - Rhodesia - Spanish Guinea - Spanish Morocco - Sudan - South Africa - Tanganyika - Tunisia - Tangier - Uganda - Italian Somaliland. (20,000 cars sold).

Australia
Australia - New Caledonia - Guam - New Zealand - Dutch New Guinea - British New Guinea (12,000 cars sold).

Asia
Aden - Burma - Ceylon - Cyprus - Hong Kong - Indonesia - Iraq - Iran - Japan - Jordan - Kuwait - Lebanon - Malaya - Pakistan - Portuguese India - Saudi Arabia - Siam - Syria - Turkey. (8,000 cars sold).

By 1963 the first of many brochures announcing the Sedan's presence across the continents on its cover had been published. *'Warum ist der Volkswagen so beliebt in 136 Ländern? Weil...'* (or 'Why is the Volkswagen so popular in 136 countries? Because...' in English language versions) screamed the headline. Such a message would remain a dominant advertising slogan for several years.

However, while some countries, most notably those in Europe, were eager, even desperate, to purchase stock, even pestering Volkswagen in advance of plans for invading yet another country had been finalised, that enthusiasm wasn't anywhere near universal. Among the most reluctant was a destination Nordhoff regarded as an absolute target, a potential revenue-raiser of epic proportions. There was also what was regarded as the home of the small car to master, a much smaller country and one that chose to drive on the wrong side of the road.

Here, the intention is to illustrate Nordhoff's initial tactics and longer term strategy to gain a substantial foothold in the lucrative US market and to demonstrate his flexibility when it came to Great Britain, probably the most reluctant to move on from the grudges of the Second World War.

The 250,000th Sedan destined for the USA was produced pre-Christmas 1958, a year when just short of 90,000 examples rolled off the assembly line specifically for American buyers.

A challenge to Detroit

Without question, in his eagerness to amass a treasury of US dollars, money that would pay for machinery, repairs to the factory and much more, Heinz Nordhoff broke his own unwritten rule of perfection and presented America with the basic Sedan of pre-De Luxe days. In January 1949 he despatched the ever-enthusiastic, super-salesman Ben Pon (forever associated with the Panel Van version of the Transporter) across the waters from his native Holland to do his very best. The trip began and ended in disaster. Thanks to a friend, Pon managed to organise a press conference on board the boat which had transported both car and salesman across the Atlantic. The publicity generated proved significant, but all of it was bad. Potential dealers simply weren't interested in such a small, spartan car; they mocked its quirky design and, encouraged by a hostile press who insisted on all calling the Sedan Hitler's car, clearly hadn't reached a point when they could forgive its Nazi forefathers for their transgressions. Temporarily deflated and despondent, the Dutchman had no option but to offload his sample car, plus a host of spare parts, on an unsuspecting victim so that his hotel bill could be settled.

As export sales spiralled, brochures tended to include at least one picture of Sedans in transit. This image dates from around 1955.

In April of the same year, the more measured and better versed in US practices Nordhoff went to America himself, but later reported his venture to have been an 'utter failure'. The car had been included in an exhibition of German products at New York's Museum of Science and Industry, but raised no interest and like Pon's 'Victory Wagon' was subsequently sold to an individual. US sales in 1949 totalled just two cars.

Not one to be dissuaded, in 1950 the Director General struck a deal with the Austrian Max Hoffman, whose Manhattan showroom was opened in 1947 and was home to the finest of European automotive exotica. Amid the razzamatazz of the PR launch, Hoffman announced it was his intention to import a minimum of 1,000 Sedans per month immediately, increasing that figure to 3,000 every thirty days in the near future. However, the reality behind the hype was that Hoffman's emporium of costly metal for wealthy individuals was totally the wrong setting for a cheap, small car. Hoffman quickly became disillusioned with the product and, more importantly, so too did his salesmen. Realistically a dismal total of just 157 cars sold in 1950 should have been enough for Nordhoff to look elsewhere, but uncharacteristically he procrastinated. Growth did ensue, but of miniscule value. 1951 saw 390 sales, while 1952 amassed a paltry total of 601 Sedans to join the others on US roads.

Somewhat belatedly, Nordhoff was finally galvanised into resolute action. Export Manager Manuel Hinke was despatched posthaste with a brief to retract the 'franchise' by the end of 1953 if Hoffman's progress didn't meet Volkswagen's target forecast. Hoffman turned on his heels, storming that the Sedan was an unsaleable commodity in the USA. Sales of just 1,013 cars appeared to justify such an assertion, but Nordhoff disagreed. If US personnel couldn't handle the Sedan, Germans already versed and successful within the Volkswagen organisation would take over.

The vastness of the United States demanded more than a single sales headquarters. Gottfried Lange from the Export Department set up his campaign tent in San Francisco, while a most interesting character, Will van de Kamp, one-time Messerschmitt pilot and

'How Volkswagen contributes to Canada's economy'. VW's subtle way of promoting the Sedan in North America.

field salesman, was despatched to New York. Lange had been selected as both a talented organiser and administrator, the non-English speaking Van de Kamp as the slightly wayward but nevertheless definitive salesman. Both men's individual form of magic worked and a flurry of dealers signed on the dotted line with the result that by the end of 1954, 6,344 sales had been made.

The following year, 1955, the point when Nordhoff would herald the arrival of the millionth Sedan to roll off the Wolfsburg assembly line, US sales rocketed to 30,298 cars. This was also the year when Nordhoff would approve changes to the Sedan's specification specifically to cater for America's needs such was its perceived importance. While Europe and beyond continued to rely on trafficators (or semaphore indicators), cars bound for the USA carried modern-style flashing indicators, as well as two-tier bumpers, their purpose being to align with those of US manufactured vehicles, thus avoiding unnecessary low speed parking damage to the cars.

In 1956 numbers increased again, this time by eighty per cent to 55,690. By the end of the decade and at a point when a future Director General took over the American operation,

Above left: New York's George Washington Bridge was a far better setting for a US Sedan than a German location. Mid-1950s.

Above right: Miami Beach, Florida. 'How does the Volkswagen go in 136 countries all over the world? It goes and goes and goes and goes and goes.' 1966.

An American view of London in 1966 presented to a British audience.

sales had increased to 150,601. Thanks in part to the work of Carl Hahn in appointing an advertising agency that broke all the rules, there would be many more sales records to come.

One significant sales milestone had already been reached, as Frank Novotny, the press chief who had successfully spun the stories of both the persona of Nordhoff as an infallible deity and the all-embracing advantages of either Sedan or Transporter ownership, had announced to the press just two days before Christmas in 1958:

> This month the 250,000th Volkswagen destined for the USA rolled off the assembly line at the Volkswagen plant in Wolfsburg. Volkswagen's exports to the US will be nearly 90,000 units in 1958.
>
> I am sending you a photo attached which shows the anniversary car on the steep section of our test site. (See the picture sent by Novotny on p. 30.)

Campaign tactics

Nordhoff's preferred method of gaining a foothold in a new market was undoubtedly one of establishing his own sales and customer services network. A prime example of such practice around the time was Volkswagen Canada Ltd, which was established in October 1952. Thoughts were also drifting towards penetrating the British market. However, not only did anti-German feelings still run particularly high in Britain, with a determination on the part of the populace to buy British wherever possible, but also the country was well known as the home of the small car.

Anyone assessing the British market at the time would soon have established that demand exceeded supply, largely due to Austin, Morris and others exporting seventy per cent of their production. Nordhoff took the decision to award a franchise to a willing taker. Here he was fortunate in that Stephen O'Flaherty, a pioneer of Sedan assembly and sales in Ireland, was eager to take on the task. Volkswagen Motors Ltd was duly established and the first shipment of cars, a modest 200 in number, arrived in Britain in July 1953.

Perhaps predictably, despite its British credentials, Volkswagen Motors Ltd sold just 945 cars in 1953 and, more alarmingly to O'Flaherty, recorded a loss of a little over £4,000. More matters of concern were to follow, as in 1954 three out of every four cars delivered to Harwich docks suffered politically motivated damage, ranging from gouged paintwork to batteries upturned and consequent corrosive acid leaks. Also, and possibly unknown to Nordhoff, the Wolfsburg factory announced that due to unprecedented demand elsewhere, it was unable to produce any more right-hand-drive Sedans for the foreseeable future. However, despite these setbacks, 3,260 cars were sold by the end of the year.

'If the Volkswagen even goes where there are no roads, how well will it go where there are roads?' Valle del Bravo, Mexico, 1966.

Volkswagen Motors Ltd's Managing Director, J.J. Graydon, packed his suitcase and made the journey to Wolfsburg to meet Nordhoff in person. The result of that appointment was the instigation, with immediate effect, of a Saturday shift dedicated to meeting the demand for right-hand-drive cars. Slowly but surely, matters improved. By 1958 sales stood at 7,436 for the year, while in 1959 a figure in excess of 9,000 was recorded. One year later and with a further substantial leap forward to over 16,000 cars sold, the Thomas Tilling Group, who had taken over Volkswagen Motors Ltd, were in a position to present the widow of Colonel Radclyffe (the head of the light mechanical industry division based at Minden and Ivan Hirst's ultimate boss) with the 50,000th car to be imported.

Above: To cater for the needs of a significant market, amendments were made to the standard specification. Note the bullet-shaped indicator on the front wing and the two-tier bumpers as depicted in this US brochure *c.* 1956.

Below: The mainstay of brochure advertising in the 1950s – stylised drawings of the Sedan – were adapted to illustrate the US specification.

5

The Millionth Beetle

Many months of preparation went into the event to mark the highly symbolic arrival of the millionth Beetle. Ninety-eight per cent of Sedans so far produced had been done so under the tutelage of Heinz Nordhoff. In 1955, the year of the millionth car, well in excess of a quarter of a million cars would be produced. By this time, neither Volkswagen nor Nordhoff were strangers to staged events presenting a garlanded car to the accompaniment of a speech from the Director General, in which he announced another production barrier had been broken.

As production of the Sedan rocketed, the marketing men saw great merit in linking the success story of the car to the dedication and achievements of the Director General. Here the workforce paraded in front of the factory to pay homage to the man nicknamed the 'King of Wolfsburg'.

The 100,000th car had rolled off the assembly line on 4 March 1950, the 250,000th by the end of 1951 and the 500,000th on 3 July 1953. Such events had become more elaborate as the achievement became ever greater. For example, the 1953 gathering included a roulette-style lottery where several random lucky employees each won a brand-new car.

Many more landmark production events were scheduled to follow after the millionth, to the extent that such events eventually became commonplace. Car number two million appeared amid the pageantry of festive spirit on 28 December 1957; the Sedan heralding three million rolled off the assembly line on 25 August 1959. Less than fifteen months later, on 9 November 1960, the four millionth car left Wolfsburg; thirteen months later on 5 December 1961, an extra bevy of troops assembled, as on this occasion the flower-bedecked Sedan was being presented to the International Red Cross. Those present were rewarded with a considerable treat as all would hear from the lips of the Director General and no other, the multiple reasons why Volkswagen had been so successful, a statement which

Sedans for as far as you can see. The large building in the distance is the factory's power station.

went above and beyond in one fell swoop what Nordhoff had previously elaborated to all but those privy to his inner sanctum.

More celebratory feats would come and go in Nordhoff's lifetime, most noticeably on 15 September 1964, by which time the figure of five million cars had doubled to ten, and in 1965, the first year when over one million cars were produced between January and December, but the Director General's speech of 1961 was never bettered. Equally significant though was his relatively infrequently repeated utterance in Stuttgart on 11 July 1954, which established that there would be no change of model or direction. These two statements and the Sperry award speech of 13 November 1958, where Nordhoff confirmed in detail his philosophy with the Sedan, contain all that is necessary to explain why the Volkswagen was and should have been named the car of the twentieth century. They also confirm why it still holds and will never lose the accolade of being the most produced car of a single type in history, and why the big celebration surrounding the arrival of the millionth was so symbolically memorable.

Volkswagen's in-house magazine, *VW Information,* carried a full-colour portrait of the Director General on its cover on the occasion of his sixty-fifth birthday in January 1964.

Nordhoff in Stuttgart, 11 July 1954

On 11 July 1954, speaking in Stuttgart, Nordhoff made one of his first pronouncements on the Sedan's future as already, despite a serious production run amounting to just five years, there were those who were speculating about the need for a new model:

> 'We are still convinced ... that the blessing lies not in bolder and more magnificent designs, but in the consistent and tireless redevelopment of every tiny detail until perfection is achieved, which is the mark of a really outstanding car and which brings truly astonishing success. Does anyone seriously believe that we would give up a vehicle type, which has for years brought us such success and so undisputedly holds the number one position in the whole of the European car industry, such that in the USA, where they certainly know their cars, it is recognised as the symbol of the German recovery? We sell the Volkswagen Sedan especially in those countries with a large, competitive and from our side, highly respected car industry, with one single argument: quality!

Nordhoff in New York at the Society of Automotive Engineers annual Sperry Award meeting, 13 November 1958

> I brushed away all of the temptations to change model and design. In any sound design there are almost unlimited possibilities – and this certainly was a sound one. I see no sense in starting anew every few years with the same teething troubles, making obsolete almost all the past. I went out on a limb. I took the chance of breaking away from the beaten path, and of doing something unusual but highly constructive for transport-hungry Europe, and not Europe alone.
>
> Offering people an honest value, a product of highest quality, with low original cost and incomparable re-sale value, appealed more to me than being driven around by a bunch of hysterical stylists trying to sell people something they really do not want to have. And it still does! Improving quality and value steadily without increasing price ... simplifying and intensifying [the] service and spare parts system, building a product of which I and every other Volkswagen worker can be truly proud, and at the same time earning enough profit, under an economic system of free enterprise, to improve production facilities with the most modern equipment ... and thus increase production and productivity every year – these things are, in my opinion, an engineer's task...
>
> I am firmly convinced that there will always be a market in this world, which we are far from covering now, for simple, economical and dependable transportation and for an honest value in performance and in quality. I am convinced that, all over the world ... there are millions of people who will gladly exchange chromium-plated gadgets and excessive power for economy, long life and inexpensive maintenance.
>
> ...Based on Professor Porsche's original design, the Volkswagen of today looks almost exactly like the prototype model that was produced more than 20 years

ago, but every single part of this car has been refined and improved over the years – these will continue to be our 'model changes' ... It has led us to success, and there is no greater justification than success, as every engineer will agree.

Nordhoff at the Wolfsburg factory – extracts from the speech made to accompany the arrival of the five millionth Sedan to be produced, 5 December 1961

We have good reason to be proud ... [the Volkswagen is] a symbol of one of the biggest industrial successes ever reached ... the result of hard, unremitting work and of diligent attention to a correctly set goal.

In defining that goal, Nordhoff précised the thought process he had engaged almost from his first day as Director General. Volkswagen's post-war mission was:

...to develop one model of car to the highest level of technical excellence.
...to dedicate every single member of staff to the attainment of the highest quality.
...to dismiss the idea that such a high level of quality can only be achieved at premium prices.
...to repress technological considerations in favour of human ones.
...to specify in the car the very highest value and to build it in a manner that will ensure it retains that worth.
...to build an enterprise which belongs to the employees more than any other industrial concern in the world.

From the nothingness Nordhoff had found on his arrival, by 1961 Volkswagen had grown to be the third largest manufacturer in the world, with only the Detroit twins of General Motors and Ford producing more cars across the world. Chrysler would vie for that third place again in 1963 but nobody had a car like the Sedan. The sceptics who didn't live through the Nordhoff era might argue that Nordhoff would have been wiser to follow the general practice of changing a model every few years. What they would fail to take into account is that throughout the 1950s and beyond, no matter how much the Director General ploughed into the organisation, demand for the Sedan outstripped supply. Who but Nordhoff's Volkswagen would use the slogan *'Es lohnt sich, auf einen Volkswagen zu warten'* (It's worth waiting for a Volkswagen)? Who but Nordhoff would spend 1,177 million Deutschmarks between 1958 and 1960 only to find that the queue for the Sedan was just as long as it ever had been?

Nordhoff said to the author Walter Henry Nelson of the situation in 1960 that 'despite a present daily production of 4,600 vehicles, the demand still can't be met, making further substantial expenditure necessary.' The millionth car was the most significant symbol of the road to success and of a car so popular that demand outstripped supply for more than a decade.

Above left: The Sedan's success story was invariably accompanied by an image of cars rolling off the assembly line.

Above right: Volkswagen's stand at the many motor shows held across Europe was invariably among the most elaborate. Frankfurt, 1958.

Celebrating the arrival of the millionth Volkswagen Sedan

> To all our dear guests who help us to celebrate the arrival of the millionth Volkswagen, the gentlemen of the press as well as the workers and employees of our own organisation and the VW dealers from home and abroad, I thank you most sincerely for coming. We celebrate this feat together out of gratitude to those who have brought about this great achievement with the work of their hands and their minds, and to give all our friends far and wide the opportunity to share in our joy. Welcome to the Volkswagen factory!
>
> (Nordhoff's preface to the millionth Sedan festival programme)

A total approaching 160,000 people attended the celebrations to mark the arrival of the millionth Sedan. Not only was the Wolfsburg factory's entire workforce invited, but so too were their families, the many distributors and dealers from across the world and crucially well over one 1,000 international motoring correspondents and journalists.

At the heart of the two-day event was, of course, the millionth car itself. The symbolism behind the act of the Director General attaching the magical chassis plate to the specially prepared car wasn't lost on anyone. A survivor, the millionth Sedan resides at Wolfsburg

Early day celebrations: the arrival of the 250,000th Sedan, 5 October 1951.

to this day and is available to be viewed by enthusiasts or those with a passing interest, alike. The millionth car carried a trim package like no other and was if anything totally out of character with the standards of Nordhoff's Volkswagen. Admittedly the choice of a metallic gold finish was skilful, one designed to glisten in the multitude of arc-lamps specially installed for the rows of press and cinema cameras. However, to make the car stand out even more the decision had been taken to add a package of diamanté trimmings which extended to the bumpers, headlamp rims, running board strips, waist or swage line and the spine of the boot lid. As for the interior, this had been fully upholstered from top to bottom with a patterned flock in startling pink.

Nordhoff's well rehearsed and meticulously polished addresses during the celebrations ranged far and wide, but all essentially told the same story. Of the total number of Sedans produced each year, on average fifty-five per cent were now destined for export. In 1955, among the top nations to succumb to the Sedan's charm and values, 35,000 De Luxe

The millionth Sedan surrounded by guests, workers and journalists.

The millionth Sedan, complete with diamanté-encrusted bumpers and headlamp rims and a smiling Director General (immediately behind the headlamp) never too far away.

examples would go to the USA, 28,000 to Sweden, 18,000 to Belgium, 14,000 to Holland, 12,000 to Switzerland and 10,000 to Austria.

'These celebrations', declared Nordhoff, 'have provided a glimpse of the world which Volkswagen has conquered and will continue to conquer.' Like any skilled orator Nordhoff had a rallying call. '[Yet] we are far from sitting on the top of the world', he declared, implying to journalists, salesmen and everyone else involved that it was their bounden duty to take home with them what they had seen and to spread the word still further.

The pageantry of dancers from Paris's Moulin Rouge; the symbolism of the spirituals performed by choirs from South Africa; the essence of the ceilidh offered by Scottish

Millionth ceremonies were almost commonplace by the time the fifth such occasion arrived on 5 December 1961. The car, 'a symbol of one of the biggest industrial successes ever reached', was presented to the International Red Cross.

dancers to the strains of accompanying bagpipes; the exciting modern brilliance of the Camino Band from South America and its accompanying throng of scantily clad girls; and the frenzied whirl of riotous colour presented by rows of Swiss nationals as they waved the flags of nations each representing a country where the Sedan had established a healthy set of roots.

Words of appreciation and thanks from export and import pioneers, from initiating assemblers and a series of adept managers, told the Sedan's rags to riches story equally well, while Nordhoff acted as the car's representative in his acceptance of the Order of Merit of the Federal Republic of Germany on the occasion of the construction of the millionth Volkswagen, to be followed by Freedom of the town of Wolfsburg, which profits made from the car had transformed from wooden shanty town to an excellent place to live.

The ultimate celebration came on 17 February 1972, when the Sedan officially took the crown as *Der Weltmeister,* the most produced car of a single type, with the 15,007,034 examples then built overtaking the Ford Model T's total.

6

Advertising the Beetle

Some writers link Nordhoff's decision to perfect the Sedan, rather than change model every few years, to the fallacy that the Director General regarded press and marketing as superfluous to the business of selling cars. Nothing could have been further from the truth. For much of the 1950s Volkswagen employed probably the most skilful artist of the day to portray the Sedan as a sleek, spacious and speedy limousine, in an exaggerated style fashionable and appealing to most manufacturers and their customers. Bernd Reuters's work, however, often put that of others to shame.

One photograph, one story contained in three small neat columns of text, revolutionised car advertising and led to the Sedan becoming a must-have purchase for the rich and famous.

Admittedly in the USA Volkswagen's marketing spend was considerably less than that of the Detroit giants, principally due to word of mouth being more than sufficient to ensure that Wolfsburg found it difficult to meet demand. Such was the alarm at Volkswagen's success among American manufacturers that by 1959 rumours were rife that they too would be producing a series of small cars.

Volkswagen of America's recently appointed Head, Nordhoff protégé Carl Hahn, decided to take action. Would reputation be sufficient in the face of a Detroit deluge and was it realistic to expect in excess of 160,000 cars to sell themselves each year forever? Hahn set about a dedicated campaign to recruit an advertising agency and, according to a near contemporary source, spent three months seeing what most would consider an excessive number of advertising executives. His choice when he made it was radical to say the least.

US advertising of the time, in keeping with the rest of the world, was dedicated to illustrations rather than photography and to lengthy accompanying wordage, cramming as many stories onto the page as humanly possible, making for less than a dynamic read. Hahn was less than impressed with the many admen he saw, all of them trotting out the same old lines; that was until he met members of the Doyle Dane Bernbach agency (known widely as DDB), then a mere infant agency with less than ten years' experience in the game.

Bill Bernbach was later to relay to author Walter Henry Nelson how all he had done was show the VW delegation ads prepared for other customers and sell them the story that DDB were advertising men who knew their business. Bernbach told VW, 'You know your business better than we'll ever know it. But we know advertising better than you do.' Hahn

Above left: A gearbox story. The Sedan was so easy to drive.

Above right: Nothing escapes the net. A story of checking what has already been checked.

loved DDB's honesty. The next stage was for a team of DDB men to visit Wolfsburg and 'talk to engineers, production men, executives, workers on the assembly line'. As a result, Bernbach:

> knew what ... [the theme] had to be. We knew what distinguished this car. We knew what we had to tell the American public ... We had seen the materials that were used. We had seen the almost incredible precautions taken to avoid mistakes. We had seen the costly system of inspection that turned back cars that would never have been turned down by the consumer. We had seen the impressive efficiency that resulted in such a low price for such a quality product. We had seen the pride of craftsmanship in the worker that made him exceed even the high standards set for him. Yes this was an honest car. We had found our selling proposition.

DDB's adverts broke with the conventions of the day. Gone were the stylised drawings, the stretched limousine capable of carrying many more than reality allowed at unimaginable speeds. In came stark photography, frequently devoid of a background, showing the car exactly as it was. Out too was the surfeit of words and multiple topics. In came an eye-catching headline and invariably three truncated columns of text telling one story per advert.

Who but DDB would risk a headline that read, 'The VW will stay ugly longer' in reference to engine life? Against a picture of a Sedan which occupied just ten per

Above left: Everything you don't need. The advantages of owning a car with an air-cooled engine.

Above right: The wit of a DDB headline sold the benefits of owning a sunroof model.

cent of the page, the tongue-in-cheek headline ran: 'It makes your house look bigger'. 'Think small', speaks for itself, but would any other manufacturer have gone ahead with a headline that read 'Lemon' against what looked to be a perfect example of the Sedan. The story was, of course, one of quality inspection. The Sedan pictured had missed the boat as the trim on the glove box lid was faulty. 'Do you earn too much to own one?' took a swipe at inverted snobbery. 'You're missing a lot when you own a Volkswagen', depicted all the unnecessary parts if the engine was air-cooled. 'Any change will be an improvement', offered a nice play on words, suggesting ugliness but in fact referring to beneath the skin advances. Possibly best of all was the one declaring that there was, 'No point showing the '62 Volkswagen. It still looks the same.' The story was of a catalogue of minor improvements, each music to the Director General's ears.

Above left: DDB's adverts rapidly morphed into full brochures, again with simple text, albeit lengthier, and eye-catchingly honest, even stark, imagery. 'Mr Howard Hoover bought the VW for a second car. Mrs Hoover liked the VW better. So Mr Hoover ended up driving their big first car...'

Above right: 'Who ever heard of a Volkswagen police car? 1965 was the year of Saint John's worst winter in years. The city's steep hills were covered with slippy slush and dangerous glass ice. But car 117 was a credit... it went uphill...'

A direct result of DDB's advertising was that when European imports tumbled as Detroit pummelled the market with its own products, there was continued growth in Sedan sales. The total number of imports fell from 614,131 cars in 1960, to just 339,160 two years later, but Sedan sales grew by 40,000 in the same period. Nor did it end there. The witty, self-deprecating style edged the Sedan towards cult status and to a point where rich and famous owners included King Baudouin and Queen Fabiola of the Belgians, Princess Margaret and Lord Snowdon, the aviator Charles Lindbergh, the actor Paul Newman and the Beatle John Lennon. What is more, Herbie lay just around the corner, the first film, *The Love Bug*, being released in the year following Nordhoff's death. The agency's interest in the VW might have started in the USA but spread across the rest of the Volkswagen world with alacrity.

'Believe it or not, this man bought a VW for its economy.'

7

'Die Neuen Käfer', August 1967

In August 1967, the start of the '68 model year, the Sedan, by now officially marketed as the *Käfer*, Bug, Beetle and many more names, was sufficiently visually different to its predecessors for Nordhoff to sanction use of the word 'new'. As a brand-new Transporter was released at the same time, the eye-catching changes made to the thirty-two-year-old Beetle design were fortuitous. Bearing in mind Nordhoff's dislike of the stylists' wish to alter a car every few years to set or follow the latest fashions, what had apparently changed his mind? The answer, of course, was nothing, for in reality every update that contributed

While the absence of photographic imagery wasn't total, the Sedan was mainly illustrated by the top-of-his-game artist, Bernd Reuters. His style, in keeping with the trend of the time, was one of exaggeration – producing a car that was longer, sleeker, more curvaceous and even shinier than reality. Here is the sunroof model. Note the extraordinary size of the roof opening. (1951)

to the '68 model year car was of a practical nature, just as they had been since the launch of the De Luxe or Export model in July 1949.

The intention here is not to discuss or list every widget and whatsit improved or replaced during the twenty-year reign of Director General Nordhoff, but rather to highlight those of significance, improvements either hidden or otherwise which would make a significant contribution to sales, be it in Germany, Europe, or across the world.

1950

Cars produced on or after 3 April featured door window glass with the equivalent of a cut-out at the top. This change was designed to improve draft-proof circulation of air and reduce likely condensation in poor weather conditions.

On 28 April production of the Sedan with a fold-back canvas sunroof manufactured by Golde began.

Photographs were often recoloured in the early days but always told a story. Here the tale is of popularity and the implications surrounding such status. (1953)

From 20 May, De Luxe Sedans were fitted with hydraulic brakes. The base or Standard model retained the cable brakes which had previously been fitted to all cars.

1951

Ventilation had remained problematic in 1950, so, with effect from 6 January 1951, ventilation flaps (known to enthusiasts as 'crotch coolers') were fitted to both front side panels.

1 April saw the addition of a bonnet-mounted Wolfsburg crest badge, a detailed enamelled emblem depicting a white castle with twin towers, a closed gate and a wolf on the battlements. Although of no practical value, the badge enhanced the feeling of a car with deluxe trim.

On 12 April, and in the same vein, a brightwork trim insert was added to the windscreen's rubber seal.

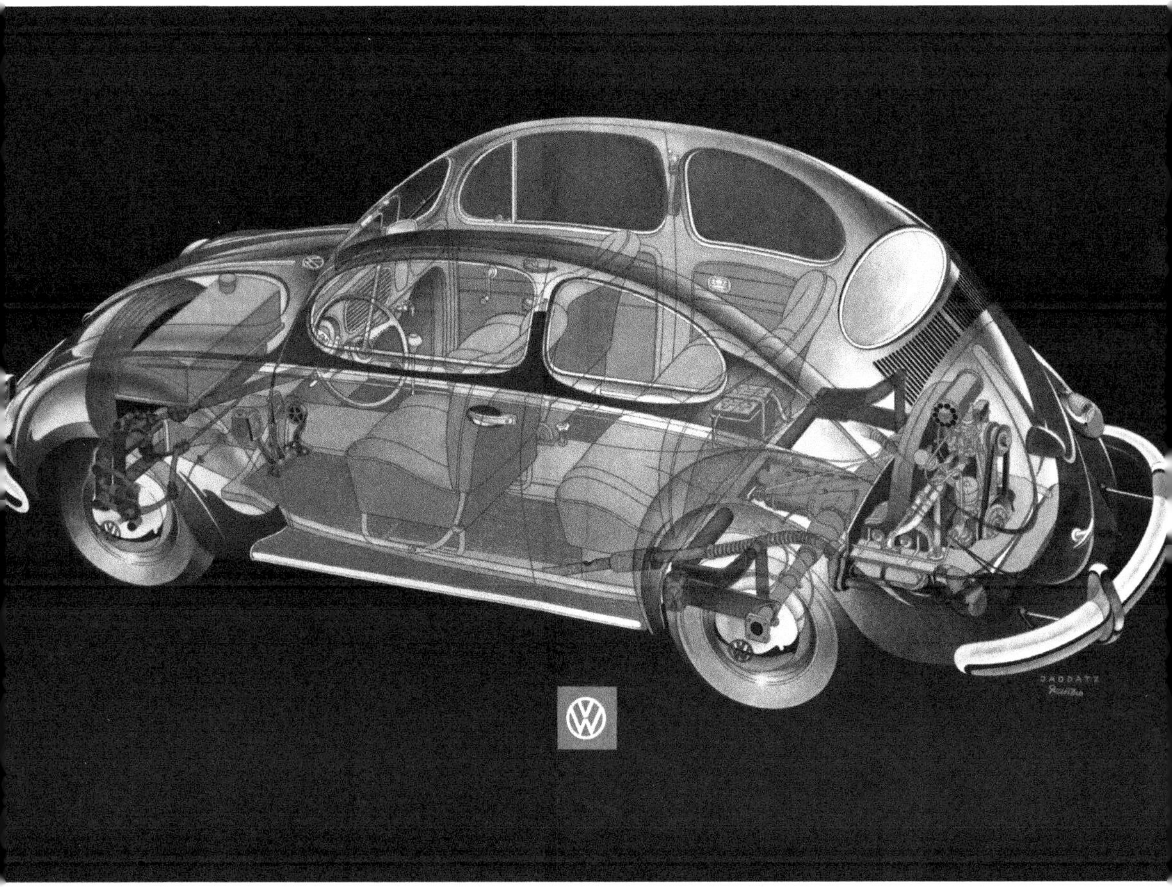

The technicalities of the Sedan were frequently presented through an illustration such as this. (1953–1955)

Whereas the makeover applied on the introduction of the De Luxe model in 1949 had been exclusively related to trim and luxury to attract new and wider markets, the changes made at the beginning of October 1952 consisted of both worthy mechanical and design improvements as well as further cosmetic trim enhancements.

Synchromesh on second, third and fourth gears was adopted but the Standard model retained cable brakes. The tyres became smaller and marginally chunkier (5.60/15 on 4J/15 rims, previously 5.00/16). Quarter lights that opened became part of the make-up of both doors ('crotch coolers' being discontinued), while wider demister vents for the windscreen, to improve air circulation and to stop demisting, were largely effective. Both the front and rear bumper took on a more substantial profile and were coupled to heavy duty overriders. Brightwork trim inserts previously only applicable to the windscreen of De Luxe cars, were now extended to the rear side windows and the split panes of the back window. The brake lights were combined with the tail lights and reflectors as a heart-shaped lens on the top of the single housing. This replaced the somewhat suspect single brake light above the licence plate which had been housed in the metalwork it shared with the bulb to illuminate the letters and digits of the number

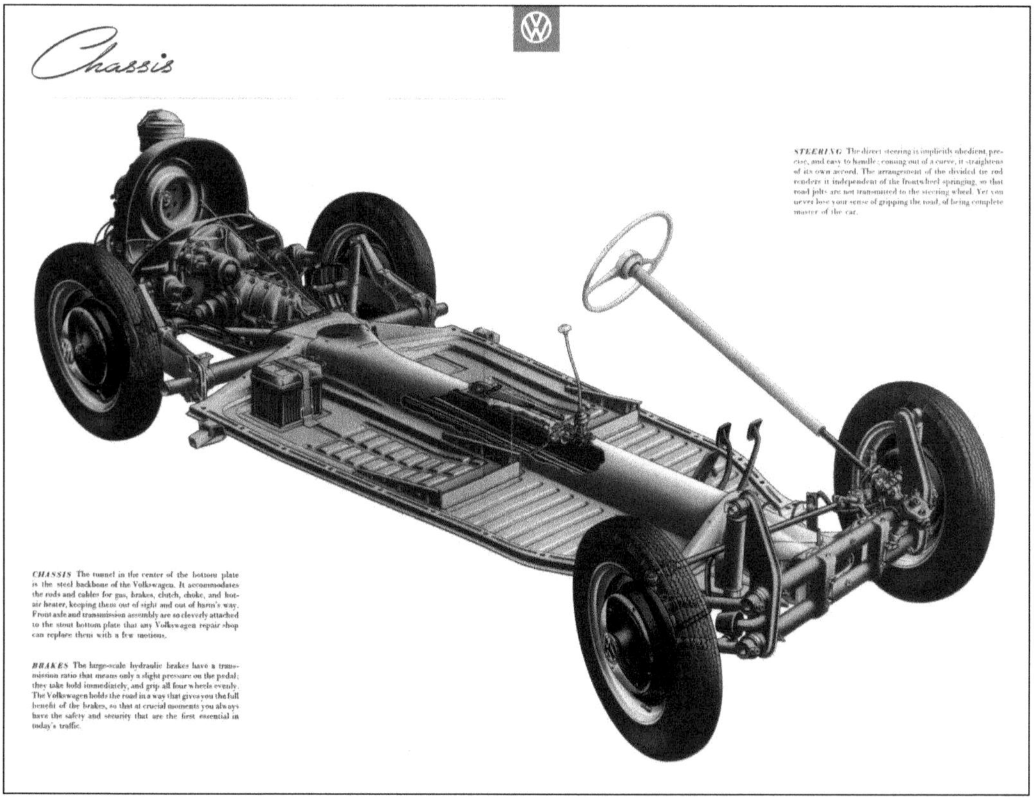

Chassis, brakes, steering and suspension were the messages behind this cleverly doctored image, which dates from the 1960s.

Suspension by torsion bars explained, but note how the underneath of a Sedan varies from that of most cars of the sixties and beyond.

plate. The windscreen wipers were given a wider sweep, while De Luxe models also benefited from a self-parking mechanism. The dashboard was completely redesigned, leading to the replacement of the previous two small open glove compartments by one larger unit complete with a privacy or security lid. The ash tray was relocated to a more convenient position for the front seat passenger while the single dial instrument housing, complete with warning lights built in, was directly in front of the driver, rather than to one side.

1953

The first significant change of the year occurred on 7 March when the size of the fuel tank filler neck was increased from 40 to 80 mm, making refuelling an easier task for the forecourt attendant. The Sedan's fuel tank was always located in the boot at the front of the car. Until the '68 model year there was no access to the fuel filler without opening the boot. This was seen as a security device, especially in the early days when theft of petrol was rife in Germany.

10 March saw Nordhoff take a hacksaw to the metal division between the split panes of the rear window. In so doing he not only increased the overall size of the new single pane window by twenty-three per cent over its predecessors, but also somehow he made the car appear more like a product of the 1950s and less Germanic in its nature.

The design of the steering wheel was amended on cars produced on or after 21 November, allowing an unrestricted view of the single instrument dial.

21 December bore witness to an increase in size of the engine. Instead of the 24 PS power unit of old with a capacity of 1,131 cm^3, both the De Luxe and Standard model benefited from 30 PS and a capacity of 1,192 cm^3. A new top and cruising speed of 68 mph was announced.

Also from 21 December the notion of separate keys for the ignition and driver's door lock was dismissed in favour of the convenience of a single one.

Sedans produced between October 1952 and March 1953 looked like these. Note the additional shiny trim when compared to earlier examples. The rear window (not visible) would have had two panes, split by a narrow strip of metal.

Towards the end of May, on the 25th to be precise, twin sun visors became standard on the De Luxe model. Previously only the driver had benefited from this everyday item.

Cars produced on or after 13 October were fitted with a shatterproof glass windscreen plus a 'clear view' circle in front of the driver.

Reuters redrew his Sedan imagery in March 1953 to show a glimpse of the new one-piece rear window. He also added 'speed' lines, implying that the 24 PS, soon to be 30 PS, engine had sports car potential.

Of greatest significance was Volkswagen's decision to change the production year to align with US practice. Previously consistent with the calendar year, from 1 August 1955 Wolfsburg started producing what they termed as 1956 model Sedans. The marketing advantage was obvious and also allowed owners to keep up with the Jones family more easily.

From 4 August onwards, the exhaust silencer became a single chamber box with twin tailpipes. The petrol tank, which remained in the boot, was nevertheless slightly repositioned and its shape altered, the aim being to increase the amount of space for luggage to be stowed. This was achieved with an increase from 70 to an 85 litre capacity.

The front seats became 30 mm wider, while the backrest was now adjustable to three different angles. The number of adjustment notches on the seat rails was increased from two to seven. Such luxuries did not extend to the Standard model. For such cars, which by 1960 accounted for just 3.4 per cent of the 725,939 total number produced, adjustment of the front seat positions remained by wing nuts.

As mentioned in chapter four, during 1955 the importance of the American market was recognised through the inclusion of parts specific to motoring conditions in the USA. 19 April saw the introduction of bullet shaped front indicators instead of semaphores, while two-tier bumpers were added specifically for America on 4 August.

The photographer behind this press shot caught the moment perfectly. The eye is naturally drawn to the new oval-shaped rear window by the smiling face looking out.

Reuters drew this image of the sunroof version of the Sedan in 1952 – note its exaggerated size. Like many an owner, in March 1953 he took his imaginary hacksaw to the bar between the two rear-window panes and created the latest look, the oval-shaped glass.

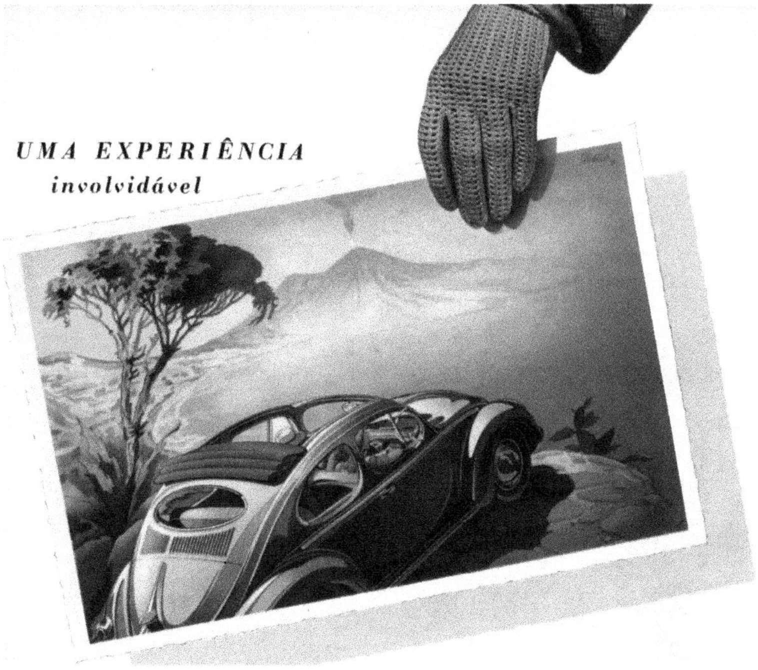

1956

During March 1956 ground clearance was reduced from 172 mm to 155 mm. Starting on 3 April, more substantial padding was used in the making of the front seats. From mid-July, all cars were fitted with tubeless tyres.

1957

To coincide with the start of the '58 model year, two significant improvements were made. Most notable was the ninety-five per cent increase in the size of the rear window. The windscreen was also enlarged at both top and bottom, resulting in a seventeen per cent increase in glass acreage and slimmer pillars. As a result of the change at the rear of the car the air intake grill contained more individual slots but equally all were more compact than previously. The engine lid was modified to assist with the mounting and illuminating of two-line licence plates. Inevitably, longer wiper blades with a wider sweep were introduced.

Inside, the design of the dashboard was completely new and sufficiently practical and appealing to remain basically unaltered on all cars (with the exception of the curved windscreen 1303 of the post-Nordhoff era) until the end of Mexican production forty-six years later. The design was aesthetically much more balanced than previously with a fifty per cent wider glove box (facing the front seat passenger) mimicking the shape of the panels surrounding the single dial (and facing the driver). The loudspeaker for the accessory radio was concealed via a grille behind the larger of two panels. The radio when fitted, or its blanking panel when not, was positioned in the centre section between the glove box and

Mixing the genres. The luxury of Reuters' car with its thickly upholstered seats matches well with the affluent young lady and her unrealistically large cargo of luggage. (1955)

Another case of doctoring – air-lines imply the 30 PS engine powers the car and its passengers at speed, despite the severity of the incline. (1955)

the dial arrangement. The central ashtray located at the bottom of the dashboard was set back, while the old arrangement of placing the ignition lock in the passenger area was improved with a move to a position in direct proximity to the steering column.

From its inception, the Sedan had carried an unusual roller type accelerator. This was replaced with an equally curious treadle-style pedal, which was covered in rubber.

With effect from 6 August, De Luxe models carried a new design of steering wheel with a deeper set hub, while the horn was operated via a semi-circular ring positioned in the lower half of the wheel's circle. The old style of pull-out door handle was replaced by a more substantial fixed handle, opened by pressing a button. Heel boards were fitted under the rear seat and a footrest for the front seat passenger was added to the specification. The front seat backrests were more steeply angled and had a deeper curve for increased comfort.

Of most significance was the tipping of the engine and transaxle assembly forwards by two degrees. This enabled the swing-axle pivot point to be lowered by 15 mm. An anti-roll bar was added to the front axle and the rear suspension was made more responsive. Nordhoff's aim was to achieve improved handling and in that he succeeded.

Why the bonnet-mounted Wolfsburg crest badge was simplified will forever remain a mystery! The wolf became red, the castle simply shiny bright, while the waves below were reduced in number.

The Karmann-assembled Cabriolet *c.* 1954; considerably more expensive than the Sedan, Nordhoff had been careful to ensure that the niche market product didn't interfere with mass production.

The start of the '61 model year, at the beginning of August 1960, bore witness to a whole host of improvements, all of which were the epitome of the Nordhoff style of striving for perfection with an existing product rather than simply casting aside and starting again.

Externally, the Sedan lost its antiquated semaphore indicators, these being replaced by top of the front wing-mounted chrome housings and orange lenses behind which a bulb flashed. At the rear of the car the rear and brake light housings were outwardly unchanged but now included an indicator bulb. Note the special lower front wing US indicators introduced in 1955 were discontinued in August 1957 and replaced by the style now available to all markets.

The fuel tank was completely redesigned with the result that the boot capacity increased from 85 litres to 140 litres.

The gearbox was redesigned and had a one-piece casing. Synchromesh was now applicable on all forward gears (but not applicable to the Standard model).

For the first time since December 1953 the engine became more powerful and now developed 34 PS. Although bore and stroke (at 77 mm and 64 mm respectively) remained as before, as did the 1,192 cubic capacity, the new engine's compression ratio of 7.0:1 (previously 6.6:1) heralded a significant increase in usable power.

A new carburettor (Solex 28 PICT) was mated with an automatic choke, which replaced the hand-operated version.

Running the engine from cold was improved by injecting warm air taken from the left heat exchanger and directing it via a flexible hose and an intake pipe to the carburettor's oil bath filter.

The space, or lack of it, available in the car can only be disguised by the rear-seat lady sitting sideways to accommodate a third and youthful passenger.

Windscreen washers became standard, although usage was hand-operated.

A sun visor for the front seat passenger became standard, as did a grab handle mounted below the windscreen and above the main body of the dashboard.

A non-repeat ignition/starter switch was fitted.

Above: The dashboard as offered between October 1952 and July 1957. Two advantages over the earlier design were the large glove box with a lid and the instrument dial's location directly in front of the driver, rather than to one side as previously.

Right: The big story for the '58 model year was a ninety-five per cent increase in the size of the rear window. Reuters was on hand and produced a brand-new drawing depicting the rear of the Sedan and, in typical manner, offered browsers a tiny back seat passenger, implying much more interior space than reality.

Probably the most significant change of the year came on 2 May 1961. In order that the rear indicator lights could be seen properly, either when the driver was braking, or driving at night, a new larger housing was introduced with a separate lens for the indicator section (orange in Europe, red in the USA).

A close second to the rear indicators and an improvement phased in on the arrival of '62 model year cars on 31 July, was the replacement with a fuel gauge of the antiquated reserve fuel tank with its flick switch when fuel was running low. The gauge had its own housing and was located at the centre of the small panel to the right of the main dashboard instrument (on a LHD car).

The boot lid was now opened and stayed open via two spring loaded struts, replacing the previous metal stay which, however, remained the specification for the Standard model.

The previous year's introduction of windscreen washers was refined with pneumatic operation.

The heel boards below the rear seat were fitted with circular shape warm air vents, while the vents in the passenger and driver compartments now came with sliding doors ensuring they could be either closed or open, the former position assisting with the demisting of the windscreen (not the Standard model).

Reuters was requested to portray the rear of the car not just on the cover of the '58 model year brochures but on internal pages too. Note this version was for the US market, hence the two-tier bumpers and the indicator housings on the wing tops.

The front seat backrest design was improved to allow a better range of positional adjustments.

Worm and roller steering replaced worm and peg, ensuring better directional control and easier operation.

Seat belt anchorage points became standard on all models.

Right: Dating from the last years of the 1950s, this cover had first seen life several years earlier when the rear window wasn't a significant marketing tool. Reuters' artwork has been duly adapted if you look closely, but the impact of the large rear window is lost.

Below: Sadly, Reuters suffered a fatal heart attack on 6 July 1958. His work lived on, other unknown artists modifying his drawings, or, as in this instance dating from 1959, re-colouring what had been a white Cabriolet and updating the bonnet badge.

On 15 April the Standard model was finally upgraded from cable to hydraulic brakes.

On 30 July 1962 for '63 model year cars, plastic replaced wool as the chosen material for the headlining. More practical and less likely to suffer the ravages of dampness, nevertheless perhaps today it may be seen as a retrograde step.

From the beginning of October the Wolfsburg crest badge was deleted from the specification. A VW emblem was added at the top end of the boot lid (close to the windscreen) as a replacement.

In December 1962 the heating system was improved by the introduction of exchangers. This replaced the old method of passing air across the hot cylinders and resulted in a guaranteed odour-free supply of warm air. At the same time the rear footwell heating outlets acquired regulating levers.

Last outing as the decade changes. Here, Reuters's original drawing has been reversed and a new driver placed in what had once been the passenger seat. Note the reference to the 34 PS engine and full synchromesh dating the issue to the '61 model year.

Rarely offered a star billing, here's the Standard model (which retained the 30 PS engine in August 1960 when other models were upgraded to 34 PS). The car is 'painted' Jupiter Grey and many wouldn't realise from the drawing that the bumpers were not chromed.

1963

On 5 August, for '64 model year cars, the fold-back canvas sunroof was replaced by a smaller all-metal crank operated roof (but this change wasn't extended to the Standard model). A further redesign of the steering wheel saw the discontinuation of the horn ring and its replacement with twin horn buttons. The licence plate bulb cover was made larger necessitating an amendment to the curvature of the engine lid.

At the end of October the casings for the top of the wing-mounted front indicators were increased in size.

A final outing for the drawing by Reuters with mid-1950s origins. The dashboard was modified by the artist, but other changes, including the body colour and revised engine lid, was the work of others.

Cars built on or after 3 August 1964, and representing the '65 model year, featured slimmer pillars, a larger rear window and side windows and a gently curved windscreen which extended 28 mm further into the metalwork of the roof panel. The windscreen was eleven per cent larger overall. The rear window was both 20 mm higher and 10 mm wider, with the result that it was almost twenty per cent larger overall, while the side windows, front and rear, were six and eighteen per cent bigger in total. The net result was much improved angle of vision. (The wiper blades were extended to accommodate the larger size of the windscreen. The sun visors were revised in shape to suit the larger windscreen and could also be swivelled to the side).

The design of the rear seat backrest changed so that it could be folded right down and secured in that position with an adjustable strap. Providing an item could be manoeuvred, either through the driver or front passenger door, this meant the car could carry considerably more luggage than previously.

The rotating heater control was replaced by two easier to use levers, one to operate the heating generally, the other to adjust the flaps regulating heat in the rear footwells. At the end of October 1964, the Standard model lost its crash-box in favour of synchromesh.

The 'technical' drawing of years gone by, now carefully revamped to illustrate, among other things, the new dashboard that had been introduced in August 1957.

The symmetry of the new dashboard of '58 model year vintage is instantly noticeable. Although modified in minor ways over the years, its basic form survived until 2003 and the end of Sedan production.

1965

For the '66 model year, starting in August 1965, Volkswagen added a new engine to the range, attributing it to the De Luxe and Cabriolet models, but not the base model. The design of this engine wasn't new, but an extra 6 PS was achieved through the adoption of the crankshaft from the VW 1500 (Type 3), the larger car introduced in September 1961. The stroke was lengthened from 64 mm to 69 mm, producing an overall capacity of 1285cc. The compression ratio was also increased to 7.3:1. The net result was a welcome increase in power of some seventeen per cent. Outwardly, cars with the 1300 engine were distinguishable by a jauntily angled '1300' badge fixed to the left-hand-side of the engine lid.

A new style of ventilated steel wheel, essentially the same as those attributed to the VW 1500, offered marginally better cooling to the drum brakes and were lighter in weight. Flat hubcaps replaced the domed style which had been in place for many years.

The semi-circular chromed horn ring was reintroduced, but was of a slightly different design.

The antiquated foot-operated dip switch mechanism was replaced by a position on the stalk to the left of the steering wheel (also used for the indicators).

The demister vents at each end of the windscreen were supplemented by a third located top middle of the dashboard (not attributed to the base model).

The front seat backrests were fitted with a lock to prevent them tipping forward.

The doors now came with safety locks which prevented them swinging open in the event of a collision.

Left: Cover of the final brochure to rely on artwork rather than photography. The year was 1960 for the '61 model year.

Below: The notion of including photographs of the Sedan in desirable locations in brochures led by artwork continued to the end of the 1950s and a little beyond. Here the message was one of air-cooled dependability whatever the ambient temperature.

The Alps – an ideal destination for a car that negotiates mountain passes without overheating and delights in wide variations of temperature.

1966

Twelve months after the introduction of the 1300 engine, a 1500 power unit was added for '67 year models. Both the 1300 engine and, after a brief interlude, the 1200, remained options; the latter for many years restricted to the base model. Although the 1493cc single port produced a mere 4 PS above the 1300, it offered a notable increase in power right across its range. The stroke was the same as the 1300's at 69 mm, but the bore was enlarged to 83 mm. The compression ratio was increased over that of the 1300 to 7.5:1. The 1500 had a cruising and top speed of 78 mph. A badge identical in style to that of the 1300 was located on the engine lid to confirm the car's top-of-the-range status.

Front disc brakes replaced drums on the 1500, but curiously this was not extended to models bound for the USA.

The rear track was increased to 1,350 mm from 1,250 mm. An equalizer spring ran transversely under the rear luggage area and was connected to each axle tube by rods and levers. This was fitted to all models for the purpose of providing extra help to the torsion bars when they were under load.

The design of the engine lid was changed to accommodate the requirements of US legislation, which demanded that the licence plate should sit as close to vertical as possible. The change, which resulted in the lower part of the lid becoming shorter than previously, also led to the creation of more space in the engine compartment.

The dashboard switches were now made of soft plastic with flat-headed knobs and finished in black to prevent reflection.

This image has been doctored, as a version also exists showing the Sedan in European market guise – no second tier to the bumper, no indicator housings to the wing tops.

A new style with simple un-doctored photographs. The date of issue was post-October 1962 as the bonnet badge had been deleted from the boot lid specification.

By this time terminology describing the base model as the Standard had been phased out in favour of the designation 1200A. However, with effect from the summer of 1966 would-be owners could also purchase a basic 1300 known as the 1300A.

(US and Canada only – 12 volt electrics and vertically positioned sealed beam headlamps. Reversing lamps mounted on the rear bumper, Volkswagen script badge on the engine lid instead of 1500).

Above: An honest value. The back cover of a 1963 model year brochure might hint that the Sedan was ideally suited to two adults and two children, rather than four grown-ups.

Right: The cover of this brochure incorporates a typical DDB agency question. The internal pages gave a multitude of answers.

The changes made to the Sedan in the summer of 1967 for the '68 model year would be the last Heinz Nordhoff oversaw. From September 1967 an automatic was added to the range primarily to satisfy the demands of the American market. For the marketing men this was the best news of all and while they were eager to label the full range of options as new, they also wanted to stress the availability of a Beetle without a clutch pedal. Readers of the previous chapter will recognise the distinctive style of the advertising agency DDB.

'Captured at a glance'. Volkswagen's latest style of technical illustration made use of an adapted photograph, hence no enhancements, *c.* 1963.

'The most revolutionary Beetle since the invention of the Beetle', screamed the headline, before adding, 'The new VW Automatic.' 'No more clutch.' 'No more gear lever. Just a selection lever.' There were plenty of themes and pithy messages:

'Outside: somewhat changed, it's true. But still a Beetle.'

'The headlights have now been moved forward a little and fitted with vertical lenses. They cast a better beam - as you'll soon see.'

'The front and the rear hoods were shortened. So you can still open them even if you do happen to dent your bumpers. And denting your bumpers isn't easy either. In fact it's quite a feat.'

'They're now much stronger than they used to be. Wider, too. And higher above the ground.'

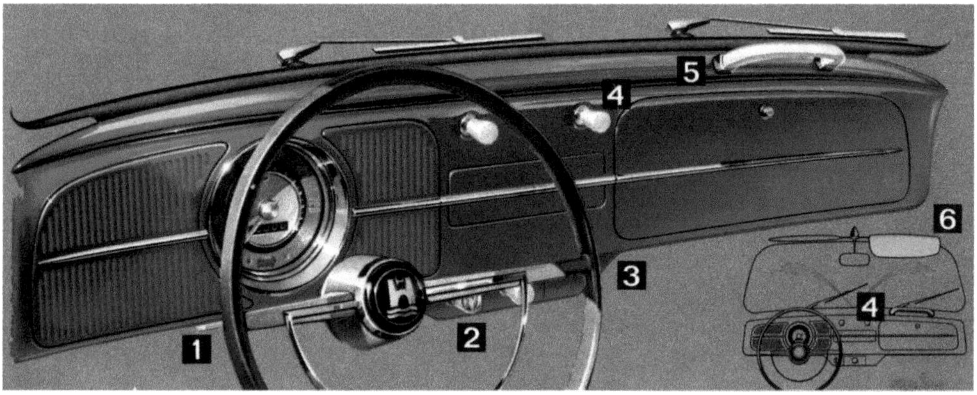

The post-August 1957 dashboard (with 1960 model year steering wheel) presented in such a way that it might be a photograph, or could be a new-look attempt to draw it as it is.

'The outside door handle's also changed. The push button has disappeared. Now there's a trigger release on the inside of the handle itself. Even less likelihood of the door springing open on impact.'

'Yet another new feature. Key-operated locks for both doors. And by the way. You no longer need to open the front hood when you want to tank. The filler neck's outside now. Behind a flap.'

1967 for the '68 model year

Significantly stronger, girder shaped bumpers, front and rear.

Engine and boot lids reshaped and shorter to accommodate the new bumpers, overriders as standard discontinued.

As the 1960s unfurled photography became more eye-catchingly original. Here, parking the Bug in the smallest of spaces made the Sedan an ideal city car across the USA.

New design for the boot handle with push button and catch hook.

Redesigned front wings to accommodate vertically located headlamps. Decorative grilles discontinued.

The central section of the boot lid closest to the windscreen has a set of louvres punched through the metal. The fresh air is directed through a box and tubes to outlets close to the windscreen.

External rear-view mirror redesigned and larger.

Interior rear-view mirror housing covered in plastic and has a safety release mechanism.

New door handles with a trigger in the handle.

The Sedan didn't need to be in the foreground of a picture to tell its story effectively.

Securing points for seat belts.

New safety steering column incorporating a crushable lattice section.

Shorter straight gear lever (previously curved).

The tank filler neck which was in the boot is now accessible externally, but is concealed by a flap door in the panel next to the front wing.

Dual circuit brakes.

The dashboard single dial incorporates all the significant warning lights and for the first time, the fuel gauge.

The 1500 automatic Beetle is fitted with a completely new double-jointed trailing arm rear axle.

12 volt electrics previously restricted to the US market become universal.

New, much larger rear light clusters with three separate coloured lenses – top indicator orange, middle brake and rear lights red, bottom (reversing light – accessory for most markets) clear.

Most of these changes were not applicable to the base model, be it with a 1200 or 1300 engine.

The '64 model year range of Volkswagens, left to right: sunroof model (with new crank-operated steel sunroof panel); the De Luxe Sedan front view; the Sedan-based Karmann Ghia; the De Luxe Sedan rear view; and the Karmann-built Cabriolet version of the Sedan.

8

A Downturn in the Beetle's Fortunes

A Machiavellian Plot

Less than four months before his death on 12 April 1968, at the age of sixty-nine, Heinz Nordhoff's praise for the car he had made his own remained as fulsome as ever. Nordhoff told an audience of importers and distributors that the '...the star of the Beetle is still shining with undiminished brightness and you see for yourselves everyday what vitality there is in this car which has been pronounced dead more often than all those designs of which hardly a memory remains'. Why then, within weeks of wresting the crown of the Director General-ship from Nordhoff, did his successor, Kurt Lotz announce that Volkswagen had been dangerously 'immovable under a single director for the last 20 years'? Why did Lotz proclaim that 'we have to move from monolith to a many-faceted product', almost as if the work of the last two decades had been futile? Why did the newcomer predict that the company's 'only chance for survival' was a 'new car'? The answer was, of course, politics.

1966 had seen the onset of the first real recession in Germany in the post-war period, which by the beginning of the following year had led to a market slump. When the inevitable cuts in production proved necessary the response of some motor manufacturers, most notably Ford and Opel, was to make great swathes of the workforce redundant overnight. Nordhoff chose otherwise. He instigated a shorter working week and launched the *Sparkäfer*, or budget Beetle, the most basic of 1200-engined cars. This was hardly the most profitable of exercises, but it did keep the workforce active, helped to stimulate sales among those always open for a bargain and enhanced the car's profile in a difficult marketplace.

Nordhoff's mistake among his laudable actions, if it should be classified thus, was to criticise the 'short-sighted' policies of the recently elected coalition government with regard to the motor industry. First they raised petrol taxes, second they allowed automobile insurance rates to spiral upwards and out of control and thirdly they denied the German worker fifty per cent of the tax concession for using a car to drive to and from work. None, steamed Nordhoff, appeared logical, but he went further, offering his own views with regard to easing the industry's difficulties. Key, the King of Wolfsburg asserted, was the abolition of car registration tax and a reduction in vehicle ownership levies.

The VW Automatic was only distinguishable externally by a badge proclaiming its status. Introduced in October 1967, this was Nordhoff's last new version of the Sedan and a car for its most important export market, the USA.

In taking up such a public sparring position, Nordhoff created a powerful enemy in the bulky shape of the apparently jovial, but unquestionably dangerous, Franz-Josef Strauss, the government's Finance Minister. His response was to attack Volkswagen and, by clear implication, Nordhoff. Hadn't VW 'hoarded vast financial reserves over many years', produced 'too many cars and too few ideas', and built 'the wrong models'? 'Two glorious initials on the bonnet of a car,' stormed Strauss, 'didn't make up for the lack of comfort.' Conscious that there had been a downturn in home market sales for the Beetle for a number of years, Strauss twisted the knife, asking what would happen 'when the USA stop being amused by the Bug?'

Strauss had two aces to play in his behind the scenes game of dirty deeds – Nordhoff could do nothing about either. In January 1964 the Director General had reached the customary age for retirement and, while outwardly he gave no signs of wishing to step down, later he was to hint that he would bow out at the beginning of 1969, a few days short of his seventieth birthday. However, it was evident that he wished to retain a controlling influence by heading the company's supervisory board. This body was a little different to the norm in Germany, in that it contained equal representation from the

Above left: Between the death of Nordhoff in April 1968 and the start of the '71 model year in August 1970, the impetus of driving sales ever-forward appeared to have lost its edge, despite huge production numbers. DDB resorted to tried and tested themes. '...People will go places they've never been before. VW's are built to take them there'.

Above right: 'In the next few years, there'll be 100 million cars on the road. But there'll always be room for a VW.'

Bonn government and the state of Lower Saxony, within whose boundaries Wolfsburg lay, as well as worker and management representatives. This body also, in theory at least, was responsible for the appointment of a new Director General in the event of resignation.

On 29 June 1966, industrialist Josef Rust had been appointed chairman of this supervisory board. The revelation that Rust was a former aide of Strauss's bestows absolute authenticity on the plot to unseat Nordhoff.

Indispensable as he might have thought himself, a man of Nordhoff's acumen wouldn't have left the matter of succession to chance. One of his protégés from the fifties, and from 1959 to 1964 the highly successful head of Volkswagen of America, had been recalled by the Director General to sit alongside him at Wolfsburg and bequeathed responsibility for worldwide sales and service. Many rightly saw Carl Hahn as the heir apparent, while Nordhoff, speaking to the author Walter Henry Nelson, as much as endorsed such thoughts with the apparently casual remark that, 'We take our promising men and send them out into the field to test them before bringing them home.' So obvious was Hahn's alliance to Nordhoff that Rust first deftly manoeuvred him away from the race to succeed, but to Volkswagen's cost, went further, eventually easing him out of the company altogether.

Dame Fortune played into the hands of the conspirators, offering them a second ace, for at this crucial time Nordhoff's health began to deteriorate. From December 1966 colleagues noticed in him a growing irritability, coupled to a remarkable loss of appetite. Under such circumstances, it appeared entirely acceptable for Rust to bring forward the appointment of a deputy and, of course, he had an ideal candidate at his fingertips. In May 1967, when Nordhoff suffered what has been variously described as a severe heart and circulatory attack, or simply a sharp decline, the fact that the arrival of one Kurt Lotz as his deputy was imminent seemed highly apposite.

Kurt Lotz was an industrialist who had worked his way through the ranks to become Director General of Brown, Boveri et Cie, a large Swiss-owned engineering firm. Opportunely, both Rust and a fellow supervisory board member, Hermann Richter, just happened to be on the board of BBC and were acutely aware that the ambitious Lotz would both toe the party line and help to ease Nordhoff out. With the Director General away from

The De Luxe, or Export, Sedan of 1949 vintage and the top of the range VW 1500 Automatic. Unquestionably the same basic car, they're parked side-by-side in 1970.

Above: The new model for the '71 model year, the 1302S, and a car given this derivation as Simca had produced a 1301, while S denoted a larger engine, namely a twin-port 1600. The 1302 without the 'S' had a 1300 engine and was only available for selected markets. Woolly thinking!

Left: 1600cc engine at the rear, but in a big break with tradition, MacPherson struts at the front of the car.

his desk nobody thought it relevant to investigate Lotz's complete novice status as far as the automobile industry was concerned.

Nordhoff's return to work in the autumn of 1967 appeared to justify the action taken despite the defects apparent in Lotz's CV. Speech proved difficult for the sixty-eight year old and increasing deafness made it difficult for him to hear all the conversations he needed to, whispered or otherwise. Those importers and distributors gathered at Wolfsburg in January 1968 to hear Nordhoff's address were to a man shocked. The Director General was barely recognisable.

Their upper hand apparent, Rust and his colleagues imparted the news to Nordhoff that for his own good his retirement had been brought forward to 21 May 1968. The Director General's reaction was to throw himself into work with apparent renewed vigour, exerting every last drop of energy he possibly could. Sadly, on 15 March on his way back from Baden Baden, where he had rushed to make yet another speech, Nordhoff collapsed. He entered Wolfsburg's hospital never to be involved with the workings of his beloved empire, cars or Transporters again.

Against the odds?

Following the slight dip in Beetle production numbers in 1966 and the more major drop in 1967, which in both instances could be attributed to the recession, 1968 saw a bounce back, with 1,136,134 million Beetles being produced, the highest figure ever; so much for Strauss, Rust and Lotz's assertions that the car's time was over. Nordhoff's legacy was that, until 1974 and the point when circumstances had changed dramatically, more Beetles left the production halls of the various factories yearly than had been achieved at any point during his reign. Was this enduring success attributable in any way to Lotz? Of course not.

Beetle production figures 1965–1974

Year	Production total	Year	Production total
1965	1,090,863 (The first year when in excess of one million cars had been produced in a twelve month period)	1970	1,196,099
1966	1,080,165	1971	1,291,612
1967	925,787 (Recession in Germany and beyond)	1972	1,220,686 (17 Feb: the Beetle becomes the most produced single model of all time (15,007,034 cars)
1968	1,186,134 (US sales rocket to 423,008 Beetles)	1973	1,206,018
1969	1,219,314	1974	791,053 (Start of Golf production: 189,890 cars)

A menu of mismanagement

Fortunately for the Volkswagen Corporation of the future, Lotz's reign can be highlighted for its brevity. During his term of four years, which tellingly was not renewed, profitability dropped considerably, from a respectable 376 million DM in 1966, to just 12 million in 1971, with nothing worthwhile to show in an attempt to explain the decline. Little, if any, progress had been made in the quest to replace Nordhoff's Beetle, while the only new model without origins in the Nordhoff era to be introduced under Lotz's tenancy did considerably more harm than good to Volkswagen's reputation. Finally, and of particular significance here, Lotz also sanctioned a change in the Beetle's make-up which Nordhoff would have been unlikely to countenance, spent a considerable amount in so doing, and reaped criticism for Volkswagen rather than reward.

Lotz's motive for the acquisition of the ailing NSU in 1969 was to get his hands on a model they had been designing for the past five years. Here, he thought, was an inexpensive way to illustrate progress to his masters and to demonstrate to the world at large that conventional water-cooling was Volkswagen's logical way forward. Unfortunately for Lotz, the K70's uncompromising three box shape was hardly eye-catching and produced an appallingly bad drag coefficient of 0.51. This in turn guaranteed poor fuel consumption. More ills lurked just around the corner, with poor engine reliability and overheating heading the list, while a little later premature and

The big story behind the 1302S was its increased carrying capacity. Unfortunately, due to the stepped nature of the boot caused by the fuel tank, the 1302S didn't have the most practical of luggage areas.

excessive rusting made this a Volkswagen like no other. To make matters worse still, Lotz could only afford to allow himself a profit margin of 33 DM per car, in order that he could sell the K70 at a price lower than that of his own luxury Audi 100. He also had little option but to decry another potential K70 rival, the VW 411, the last of Nordhoff's cars, a model launched after his death, but developed in his lifetime. His description of the largest of the air-cooled VWs as 'no metal Adonis' was typical of Lotz's ability to shoot Volkswagen in its own foot.

Lotz's imperious declaration that 'Wolfsburg will never see the 20 million mark ... we won't repeat Ford's mistake', summarised his target to rid Volkswagen of the Beetle. To this end he carefully purged himself of the majority of Nordhoff's management team within less than twelve months of the original Director General's death. Having cast aside both experience and knowledge and reducing the average age of the board from sixty-two to forty-seven, he also appointed a new man, Werner Holste, to take over the technical reigns at Wolfsburg, overlooking his background in general mechanical engineering and, as a result, a set of skills at odds with what was required. Needless to say, when Lotz was shown the door all that existed was a mishmash of ill-thought-out ideas and an occasional unsuitable prototype, most of which had originated at the Porsche design studio.

The not so super Super Beetle

That the preferred designation of 1301 for Lotz's new variation on the Beetle theme couldn't be adopted, as it had already been used by French manufacture Simca, is representative of this shambolic period in Volkswagen's history.

Introduced in August 1970, the reason for producing the 1302 Beetle remains something of a mystery. Certainly, those examples designated 'S' sported an engine new to Beetles for German consumption: a 1584cc unit borrowed from Nordhoff's second generation Transporter of August 1967 vintage. However, this engine had already been installed in traditional straight-forward US models for a twelve-month period. Press releases had told US citizens a story of a 'slightly larger engine giving it greater response and more rapid acceleration'. However, a standard 1302, not readily available in all markets (including the USA and Britain), carried a twin-port version of the 1,285cc engine of the 1300, as introduced in the summer of 1965 and still a readily available option in conventional guise. Was somebody already voting with their feet?

What was different and exclusive to the new model 1302 was its front end. Out was Ferdinand Porsche's legendary rugged torsion bar suspension, its place taken with conventional MacPherson struts. To accommodate the attendant coil springs, 'towers' had to be incorporated, which in turn had the effect of altering the shape of the wings, making them more bulbous. To complete what detractors chose to call the 'pregnant' Beetle, there was a wider and longer boot lid, and as a result a car with a distinctly unpleasant humped frontal appearance.

Marketing were directed to shout about the 1302 Beetle being faster, more 'exciting' and the 'most comfortable' ever, each accolade allegedly justifying the title of Super Beetle. They also had to excuse the millions of Deutschmarks spent on creating a larger luggage space,

Above: Volkswagen's marketing office in Britain produced this publicity image of the 1302S, a picture which shows the humped nature of the front end particularly well. The shape led to the nickname of the 'pregnant' Beetle.

Left: August 1972 saw the launch of the 1303 Beetle, essentially a 1302 with a curved windscreen and a moulded plastic dashboard. The car pictured is a US model, identifiable by the extra-large indicators on the front wings.

which was apparently Lotz's real reason for meddling with the car. Yes, the size of the boot was increased by eighty-five per cent, from 140 litres to 260 litres, mostly due to the redesign allowing the spare wheel to lie flat rather than near vertically. However, the increase in space didn't make it an easier car to load, as to accommodate the petrol tank which resided there the boot had to be stepped. Similarly, 260 litres was still paltry. As a pertinent comparison, without interfering with the rear bench seat of the first Golf, that car offered 370 litres of boot space.

Lotz offers a final faux pas

Disliked by the diehards, nevertheless, as the production figures show, the 1302 sold well. However, Lotz heard a whisper that there was a distinct possibility that in the US a law might be devised stipulating a minimum distance between the driver or passenger and the windscreen. The equivalent of a green paper in Britain confirmed that if what was planned came to fruition, the Beetle with its diminutive acreage of dashboard and near flat windscreen wouldn't comply.

Panic stricken, Lotz immediately commissioned work to be done that he thought likely to save the day. The result, the 1303, was the most un-Beetle-like Beetle ever: a car with a much shorter boot lid and a considerably larger curvaceous windscreen, which was directly linked to the heresy of a substantial moulded plastic dashboard. Here was a design of the thirties, an outstanding success of the fifties and sixties, melded with a key characteristic of the plastic age of the seventies and beyond.

See the 1303 Beetle. With a smart, sporty dashboard.

Purists horrified by the arrival of the 1302 were distraught when they saw the 1303's modern dashboard, a moulded plastic creation designed to satisfy pending US legislation – laws which never materialised.

The 1303 was launched exactly ten months after Lotz had been escorted out of Wolfsburg's back door and at the point when a decline in demand for the Beetle was first noticeable. Needless to say, Lotz's needn't have bothered to develop the 1303, as the proposed regulation that panicked its birth never came to fruition.

The end for the Beetle?

Lotz's successor, Rudolf Leiding, was a very different kind of animal. A trainee of the Nordhoff school, he was a former President of Volkswagen do Brasil and Board Chairman of Audi NSU Auto Union AG. Whereas Lotz had shilly-shallied, Leiding moved swiftly and determinedly, his aim to have a full range of new cars on the market as quickly as possible. A percentage of Beetle devotees have long considered this man more than any other to be the enemy of their pride and joy, but Leiding, however brusque he might have been, realised that if the Beetle had a future at the centre of Volkswagen when Nordhoff died, that position had been so badly undermined in the Lotz era that a return was impossible.

In the latter years of German Sedan production, Volkswagen opted to release a series of models with extra trim features. The cars photographed here are examples of the US's *La Grande Bug*.

The story of his introduction of the larger, family car VW Passat, the presumed Beetle successor Golf, the sporty Scirocco and due to inflation the real Sedan replacement Polo (in that order) isn't relevant here, save to say that during his tenure of office no new initiatives were considered for the Beetle. Instead, to make way for production of the Golf, on 1 July 1974 Leiding ousted the Beetle from its Wolfsburg assembly line, transferring production to Volkswagen's Emden plant. 11,916,519 Beetles had been built at Wolfsburg. It is also likely that Leiding was the man behind the '76 model year scaling down of the Beetle range, with just a basic 1200, a deluxe version of the same car marketed as the 'L' (and available in one or two markets with a 1600 engine), and the Karmann-assembled Cabriolet, surviving the purge.

If this final act was really of his making, perhaps at least a basic course in villainy should be added to his CV, for while it can easily be argued that to axe the un-Beetle-like 1303 was logical, to deprive the Sedan in tin-top mode of all but the now decidedly underpowered 34PS, 1200 engine across great swathes of the world was deliberately brutal, almost forcing those loyal to the VW emblem to purchase a new generation car.

Perhaps Leiding had carefully planned the fate of the old master, a destiny that would see it survive for many years to come: we simply don't know. Leiding was called upon

Following the decision to axe Sedan production in Germany, diehards were catered for with cars built in Mexico. All were powered with the 34 PS engine and featured the flat screen and torsion bars of the classic Volkswagen. A series of special edition models boosted sales. This is the Aubergine Bug. The large rear light clusters had been a feature of all cars built part-way through the '74 model year and later.

to fall on his sword at the beginning of 1975, health issues being cited, but in reality profitability, or the lack of it, being the root cause. The lingering effects of the oil crisis of 1973 and global recession couldn't have come at a worse time for Volkswagen. To bring a swift transition from air to water-cooling, Leiding had had no option but to spend heavily. In 1974 Volkswagenwerk AG recorded a loss of 555 million DM and was destined to stay in the red the following year.

Life after death

At midday on 19 January 1978 the very last tin-top Beetle to be built on German soil was ushered off the Emden assembly line, the 16,255,500th such example. Worldwide total production by this time stood at 19,300,000 and it was thanks to the cars assembled in locations other than in Europe, most notably Mexico and Brazil, that Lotz's imperious claim that the twenty millionth Beetle would not be seen, was proved erroneous. Amazingly, cars identical to that milestone special edition Silver Bug which had rolled off the Puebla, Mexico, assembly line on 15 May 1981, were on sale in selected countries of mainland Europe's VW dealerships. Sadly, right-hand-drive Britain and, for that matter, legislation riddled and cocooned America couldn't be catered for.

A part of the final consignment of 3,150 Sedans shipped from Mexico to Germany in August 1985. Known as the Jubilee model, decals proclaiming *50 Jahre Käfer* marked the fiftieth anniversary of the original design.

Recognising that in the Beetle Volkswagen still had something special, the latest Director General, Toni Schmücker, had sanctioned the import of Beetles from Puebla to replace the home-built product. Unlike the seemingly maverick Brazilian operation, whose Beetles carried a strange mixture of parts and panels from a spectrum of German production years, the Mexican Beetle illustrated few differences from the German 1200L – a slightly smaller rear window, a flat rather than humped rear valance and a DC generator instead of an AC alternator being the most notable exceptions. The fact that the Mexican car featured the 34 PS engine was not an issue domestically and thanks possibly to Leiding's foresight, didn't come as an unexpected horror to would-be owners in Germany.

When sales of the Mexican Beetle in Germany are compared to those of the car in its heyday, it is easy to see how much Volkswagen had changed. West Germans registered 10,876 Beetles in 1978 and 14,650 the following year. By 1982, however, this kind of figure had tailed away to 6,271 and the writing appeared to be on the wall. A tactic of the seventies was employed with a succession of special trim models, a move which paid off, with sales rising to 12,622 cars in 1983 and 11,061 the following year. Predictably, a dismal 5,087 sales in 1985 led to the latest Director General announcing enough was enough. Sales shot through the roof immediately, particularly as the last edition model offered devotees a particularly attractive package ingeniously linked to the fiftieth anniversary of Porsche's first *Volksauto* prototypes.

By a curious twist of fate the man who finally banished the Beetle to a permanent exile in South America was none other than Nordhoff's protégé, Carl Hahn, the man behind the car's achievement of cult status in the USA in the 1960s. He'd returned to Volkswagen as Director General in January 1982.

Production of the Brazilian-built Sedan, known as the *Fusca*, came to an end on 7 December 1986, but was later revived for three years thanks to government intervention and monies – finally ending on 11 July 1996.

Mexico's involvement with the Beetle stemmed from 1954 when the first cars were imported. Government intervention ensured a quick transition to CKD assembly and over the years local content grew steadily. In 1966 a brand-new manufacturing plant was established at Puebla, a city of some three million inhabitants some 80 miles south-east of Mexico City. Although the number of cars produced annually never rose to anywhere near the lofty heights of German production, or for that matter the operation in Brazil, it was always worthwhile. In 1967, 17,630 Sedans were produced, while by 1970 this figure had increased to 35,303, until in 1974 numbers had more than doubled again, this time to 77,391. Although a decline linked to one of Mexico's frequent financial crises followed, by 1978 production stood at a respectable 51,697 cars, a figure boosted by exports to Europe.

Many years after leaving Volkswagen, Rudolf Leiding endorsed the Beetle's position in Mexico. 'It is undeniable,' he said, 'that for Mexico the Beetle was the ideal automobile. In this country, where the paved roads ended and other models failed, the Beetle kept right on going towards its goal ... in this market the Beetle had displaced its competitors.' Anyone choosing to follow *El Vocho's* (little child) or *El Escarabajo's* (scarab beetle, a symbol of immortality) progress over the years between 1985 and 2003 and its eventual demise, will appreciate that Puebla had employed Nordhoff's highly unusual, but equally successful, tactic of improving the car year-by-year, rather than being led by those 'hysterical stylists' he'd so roundly condemned all those years earlier.

Free of the restraints of catering for the German market, the Mexican Sedan evolved, albeit in a conservative manner. With demand for retro designs surging in Europe, unfortunately nobody thought of reviving sales of the Beetle, despite its modern-look makeover. The car depicted here dates from the 2001 model year.

This is not the place to itemise every widget type change, but it is worth recording the most significant developments illustrating Beetle near immortality. In 1987 the wipers were offered with an intermittent wash-wipe facility. By 1988 a 1600 engine was standard and to this was added electronic ignition. Dual circuit brakes were added from October 1991, while a year later Digifant fuel injection was introduced. In 1994 front discs replaced the less effective drums. By the mid-1990s, the 1600i engine as it was branded, offered maximum power of 44PS at 4,000 rpm from its fuel-injected, catalytic converter-suppressed 1584cc engine. The compression ratio was 7.7:1 and maximum torque stood at 94 Nm at 2,200 rpm. Fuel economy hovered at just over 40 mpg. Admittedly acceleration from 0–60 mph in 17 seconds was hardly record beating, but a top speed of 95 mph was distinctly acceptable.

Beetle aesthetics were similarly attended to, with a first modification post-German era change of significance coming in 1987, when the colour of the headlining was changed from white to blue (and two years later to suitably palatable soft grey). Following the general trend to abandon chrome and brightwork, the front lid lost its trim strip in 1992, while three years later the already wider upgraded bumpers became colour-coded, as did the headlamp trims. Concurrently, fashionable black replaced chrome or aluminium on items such as the door handles, the surrounds of the front side windows and even the bonnet-mounted VW roundel. In 1985, the one-time bright trim strip on each side of the car was scrapped, having been swopped over to black earlier. Hubcaps were sprayed rather than chromed and by 1997 the VW roundel had been dispensed with.

From a low point of 16,746 Beetles built in 1986, the year after exports to Europe ceased, sales flourished. By 1990 84,716 cars were manufactured for home consumption in the twelve-month period. Puebla rejoiced in the production of the twenty-one millionth Beetle produced worldwide on 23 June 1992. The following year they produced an astonishing 98,236 cars. Sadly, a severe economic depression coupled to drastic repeated devaluations of the peso ensued, resulting in just 15,933 Beetles being produced in 1994. However, by the dawn of the new millennium and sixty-five years after the appearance of the first prototypes, Puebla contributed a further 41,260 Beetles to the cumulative total. However, from this point a decline set in with figures of 38,850 and 24,007 in 2001 and 2002 respectively. When by the middle of 2003 only 7,500 Beetles had been built and legislation had come into force banning the Beetle as an appropriate vehicle for use as taxi, all knew the end was in sight. On Thursday 10 July 2003 an announcement was made confirming the Beetle's fate and production of 3,000 *Última Edición* Beetles commenced immediately. On Wednesday 30 July car number 21,529,464, an Aquarius Blue example laden with retrospective trim as befitted the end of an era, was eased from the assembly line, its windscreen plastered with the message, '*Volkswagen de México Último Sedán del Mundo 30 de Julio 2003*' ('Volkswagen of Mexico Last Sedan in the World July 30, 2003').

Volkswagen do Brasil

Volkswagen's Brazilian operation was established early in 1953 and immediately began the task of assembling CKD Beetles and first-generation Transporters. As early as 1957 full manufacture began in a purpose-built factory at Sao Bernado do Campo, near São Paulo. By 1959 these cars consisted of ninety-five per cent Brazilian content. Gradually the German

Beetle and the Brazilian product began to drift apart, as the former developed and the same course was not followed in São Paulo. One very obvious example of this divergence came in 1965 when German Beetle windows, front, rear and sides were increased in size. Volkswagen do Brasil didn't follow suit and never would. Other instances include disc brakes, a part of the specification for the new 1500 Beetle in Germany in 1967, which only arrived in Brazil in 1973. Dual circuit brakes weren't a part of the makeup until 1978. Rear swing axles were never upgraded. Between 1960 and 1973, the Brazilian cars sported wheels which bore a similarity to those of the Porsche 356. When the 1600 engine was introduced in 1976 it came with twin carburettors, while smaller 14-inch wheels were standard. In 1978, the Brazilian Beetle adopted its own unique style of steering wheel, while a few years later it carried a padded dashboard with exclusive square-dial instruments.

'Each *Vocho* has a story, and each story has an ending.' For the Mexican Sedan, that day came on 30 July 2003 at a point when 21,529,464 examples had been built.

These and many more divergences from the Beetles built at Wolfsburg, Emden, or even Mexico, ensured that when Schmücker decided to satisfy the demands of the European diehards and import cars from a still active manufacturing plant, São Paulo couldn't be considered, despite production way in excess of all others.

By 1966 the Brazilian operation employed 11,000 workers and sales accounted for sixty-two per cent of all cars sold in the country. On 4 July 1967 the 500,000th Beetle rolled off the South American assembly line. Less than five years later that number had doubled and, in March 1972, the millionth *Fusca* (the Portuguese word for Beetle) had emerged. Two years later, annual production had risen to 237,323 cars, 24,500 of which were exported. Mid-1976 saw the 2,000,000th Beetle, while exports extended to some sixty countries across the world.

Disappointingly after such a long reign, as the 1980s started to gather pace, interest in the Beetle began to falter. By 1984 home market sales had slumped to 34,000, so it was with a degree of inevitability that it was assumed that the last Beetle ever to leave the São Paulo assembly line had done so on 7 December 1986, at a point when total *Fusca* production had reached in excess of 3,321,000 cars. However this was not to be the case. In 1993 the Brazilian President, Itamar Franco, impatient not to lose the votes of an emerging class of voters eager to own a car for the first time, demanded that the government should avoid a damaging upsurge in cheap Japanese imports by allowing the state-funded car industry, Autolatina, to assist with the reintroduction of the home-built Beetle at a subsidised price. Once back in production at a rate of 200 cars per day it was soon discovered that older, more affluent people were also eager to own the robust Beetle as a second car, useful on the rougher roads which were plentiful. Suddenly, the future looked rosy once more.

Sadly, just three years later, a change in government policy that brought an end to those much-needed tax incentives to make production feasible resulted in manufacture coming to a halt once more on 11 July 1996. This time it was to be forever.

Footnote – the Beetle that wasn't

In 1997 Volkswagen introduced the quirky and somewhat impractical New Beetle. Outwardly, it bore more than a passing resemblance to the original, but that is where all similarity ended. Based on the platform of the VW Golf Mk 4, this front-wheel-drive car had its water-cooled Golf engine at the front and a small luggage area at the back and was an excellent example of a manufacturer producing a car with in-vogue retro appeal based on a popular car of a previous era. Like many a fashion, interest eventually waned, a second version of the new Beetle seeming to offer less appeal, and in 2019, production ceased.

Bibliography

Barber, Chris, *Birth of the Beetle* (Sparkford: Haynes Publishing, 2003)
Copping, Richard, *Great Cars Volkswagen Beetle* (Dorchester: Veloce Publishing, 2018)
Copping, Richard, *VW Advertising, The art of selling the air-cooled Volkswagens* (Shebbear, Devon: Herridge & Sons Ltd, 2014)
Copping, Richard, *VW Beetle Specification Guide 1949–1967* (Ramsbury: The Crowood Press, 2018)
Copping, Richard, *VW Beetle Specification Guide 1968–1980* (Ramsbury: The Crowood Press, 2010)
Etzold, H. R., *The Beetle – Production history of the people's car* (Sparkford: Haynes Publishing, 1998)
Ludvigson, Karl, *Battle for the Beetle* (Cambridge MA: Robert Bentley Publishers, 2000)
Nelson, Walter Henry, *Small Wonder, The Amazing Story of The Volkswagen* (London: Hutchinson & Co. Ltd, 1970)

Acknowledgements

The author and publisher would like to thank the following people/organisations for permission to use copyright material in this book: all pictures copyright Volkswagen Aktiengesellschaft. All pictures sourced from Volkswagen Aktiengesellschaft.

With many thanks to fellow VW enthusiast Keith Bolton for encouraging progress towards the completion of this book and for painstakingly reading and correcting each chapter as it was written.